DEALING WITH THE DEVIL

WARNING

It is only fair to warn you that Satan HATES this book. He doesn't want you reading it, for he knows what it will do in your life. Some Christians have said... "This is the hardest book I've ever tried to read." And it's not because the reading is difficult, but because the satanic opposition is so fierce.

From the moment you first sit down to read, you can expect interruptions of every kind. Phone calls, special errands, unexpected demands on your time, plus a stream of distracting ideas bombarding your mind. If you watch for these things, you'll almost find yourself laughing as you behold Satan's panic.

Now some, of course, have no trouble at all. But they are a minority. Most readers tell us they have to resist the devil to get through the book. This warning is NOT meant to discourage you. It should EXCITE YOU to think you have something so powerful in your hands that the devil doesn't want you to read it. So brush aside his distractions and get ready to absorb some know-how that will change your life...as it changed mine.

C. S. L.

DEALING WITH THE DEVIL

by C. S. LOVETT
M.A., M. Div., D.D.

author of
"HELP LORD—THE DEVIL WANTS ME FAT!"
LATEST WORD ON THE LAST DAYS
SOUL-WINNING MADE EASY
LONGING TO BE LOVED
president of Personal Christianity

ILLUSTRATED BY LINDA LOVETT

published by
PERSONAL CHRISTIANITY CHAPEL
Box 549, Baldwin Park, CA 91706

1984 edition

ISBN 0-938148-05-2

CONTENTS

WHY...

"PUT ON THE WHOLE ARMOUR OF GOD!"
Eph. 6:11

IF THERE IS NO ENEMY?

The **HEART** of this book is a PERSON — SATAN.

The **OBJECT** of this book is to prepare Christians for spiritual encounters with the devil and equip them to **RESIST** him.

The **PREREQUISITE** of this book is an unquestioned acceptance of God's Word where it speaks of the EVIL ONE.

The **SUCCESS** of this book depends on the reader's willingness to **TEST** what he reads by the Spirit of God and **TRY** the mechanics in Jesus' name.

NO ONE TOLD ME

I was saved by "accident."

In 1947, a ridiculous circumstance took me to a minister's conference. I didn't want to go, but a Presbyterian friend tricked me into it. He thought I was saved and that the conference would involve me in Christian service. I was bored stiff with the lectures.

During a break I sat by myself at one side of the auditorium. "How in the world did I get into this mess?" That's what I was asking. Then I began to overhear a group of men talking. Standing about eight feet in front of me were five of the conference speakers having a private huddle. Today I know them; Dr. Bob Pierce, Dr. Harold Ockenga, Dr. Richard Halverson, Dr. Armin Geswein and Dr. Robert Boyd Munger. They were discussing the mechanics of salvation and I was eavesdropping. By God's "accident," they talked of things I needed to know. Thank God for those men!

WHAM! The light went on! I heard what I needed to hear.

I couldn't wait to get home and explain it to Margie, my wife. We knelt together in our living room and asked Jesus to come into our hearts. He did. It was wonderful. I had been wandering in spiritual darkness for years.

All those years and no one troubled to explain the mechanics to me. It upset me to think that salvation was as simple as talking to Jesus. Simple, yet no one told me how to meet Christ alive. God used my annoyed spirit to produce **Soul-Winning Made Easy.** Many of you know about that. The "accident" of my salvation was His way of bringing forth the "Encounter-Method of Soul-Winning."

Then it happened again!

The first 20 years of my Christian life no one told me about Satan. I didn't dream that there was a **personal** devil, any more than I suspected Jesus was a **personal** Savior. How could I know there were spiritual mechanics for dealing with him just as there are for dealing with Christ? I didn't know there was anything I had to **do** about Satan any more than I knew I had to do business with Jesus to be saved. No pastor, no professor at seminary, no friend in Christ ventured to explain our greatest enemy.

Didn't I know the doctrine of Satan? Of course, I knew that. I also knew from childhood about Christ. My Bible college and seminary training was thorough in traditional Satan data. I believed in him like Columbus. I would say with other Christians, "The devil sure got in

9

that time!" This was how we would explain an unfortunate situation. But it was just a cliché, a Christian expression. The **fact** of Satan was unquestioned. But the **presence** of Satan was something else. I discovered it by "accident." You'll read about that shortly.

● Once again the Lord "upset" me with an obscured truth. Why so much vagueness in the Christian's experience with Satan? Why no clear-cut explanation, no mechanics for dealing with this one who plagues our lives? No wonder Christians have trouble living for Christ. Their greatest enemy is left unmolested!

My motive for writing this book is **your victory over Satan.** It is not a devotional manual. It is not Godward, but Satanward. If you find a point or two which appear to be upsetting, please believe I want only for you to regard Satan as your **personal** enemy and to **equip you with a means** for resisting him. After reading this book, you'll not be able to say. . .

"NO ONE EVER TOLD ME ABOUT SATAN!"

HE LIVES...
SATAN THAT IS!

I saw the devil at work and it shook me.

The occasion was a strategic meeting of a well known foundation with people of the translating and publishing committees for a new translation of the Bible. It was a critical session for bringing a new work to the world. Momentous decisions were before the foundation's directors.

With remarkable timing, a person present spoke words which stabbed the president of the foundation with anguish. I saw the hurt of his soul rise to his face. The spirit of the meeting changed instantly. All decisions were deferred.

 Now the one making the comment was a friend of mine. He is as gracious and godly a Christian as you'd hope to meet. Those words from his lips didn't sound like him at all. When I saw how his wonderful spirit had dramatically changed and beheld the great damage wrought in the president, I was perplexed — "How could such a thing happen?"

The rest of the meeting slipped by. I sank into my chair to reflect on this amazing disruptive spirit. What in the world possessed _____ to say such a thing? It sounded like someone else. But who? The Holy Spirit moved within me. Indeed, someone else had authored that comment — SATAN!

The instant that truth struck, I trembled. The palms of my hands became sweaty. A dreadful awareness swept over me. I experienced something about Satan I hadn't realized before. No one heard the gospel tune that rang within me, but a shout was echoing . . .

HE LIVES, HE LIVES
SATAN LIVES TODAY
HE WALKS WITH ME AND
TALKS WITH ME, ALONG
LIFE'S NARROW WAY!

I heard that. It began to haunt me.

A SATANIC SLIP?

I drove from the meeting practically overcome with the reality of Satan. I'm sure he didn't plan that, for his effectiveness requires absolute secrecy. But something happened this day to give him away. He didn't slip, he's too wiley for that, but God, working in grace, directed my eyes to the Evil One. For the first time in my life Satan was more than a doctrine — **He was a danger.**

I thought back to seminary days when I had to present the doctrine of the devil on paper to my professors. How easy it was to collect the Scriptures referring to his person and work. It felt good to recite the passages, a sort of protective feeling went with it. Like most Christians, I took great comfort in, ". . . greater is HE that is in you, than he that is in the world" (1 John 4:4). I regarded that statement as **automatic armor** against the "wiles of the devil." Somehow I felt **shielded** just thinking the Almighty lived within me.

But then . . . He also lived within the two brethren just fallen prey to "the firey darts of the Wicked (One)" (Eph. 6:16). That shielding **couldn't be so automatic.** An inspired thought entered my soul: "What would my doctrine of Satan look like translated into experience? Would I recognize it?" Doctrines in action often look differently. After the experience that day, I was to get serious about Satan. He was more than a doctrine now — he was a **living person!**

WATCHING FOR SATAN

It's one thing to discover Satan alive, another to know what to do about it. Only one place I knew to go — God's Word, the rock of my life. I needn't tell you the Scriptures jumped. It's like when you own a motor home, you suddenly notice all the motor homes on the road.

The Word of God was quickening my soul. It was getting clear. The Bible told me to WATCH for Satan. But of course I hadn't. Nobody else was watching for him. I had never heard anyone say much about it one way or the other. So he simply remained a doctrine to me. Be-

13

sides, I wouldn't have known **HOW** to watch for him. Bible truths loomed up describing Satan as:

> **An Angel of Light** (2 Cor. 11:14)
> **An Adversary** (1Peter 5:8)
> **A Tempter** (1 Thess. 3:5)
> **A Deceiver** (2 Cor. 11:3)
> **A Hinderer** (1 Thess. 2:18)
> **A Beast** (Rev. 19:19)
> **A Restless Lion** (1 Peter 5:8)
> **The God of this World** (2 Cor. 4:4)
> **Prince of the Power of the Air** (Eph. 2:2)

If I had an enemy who was all those things, it was time I found out what his operation looked like. I had just seen him work in an important meeting, but I had never **SEEN** him work in me. At least not to **recognize** it as it **happened.** How fabulous it would be to catch Satan in the act! If I could do that, I might learn something about his methods. What a terrific thing it would be to become skilled in **anti-Satan methods!** Wow! That's big stuff!

So I determined to become a Satan watcher.

This was the beginning of tremendous victory in my life. I did catch him and still do. And through it, I have learned a wonderful, practical way to deal with him. Consequently, one of the most precious verses in the Word of God for me, is . . .

 "Resist the devil and he will flee from you" (James 4:7).

You can't imagine what it is like when Satan FLEES! It is glorious! Yes, he comes back and there is no bottom to his bag of tricks, but what a moment when he flees! If you haven't tasted it, you must. I don't want any Christian God allows me to reach, to go through

14

this life without knowing the thrill of that moment. I have found it to be the key to victory in the Christian life.

FOR BIBLE BELIEVERS ONLY

It is not my purpose to write for those questioning or doubting God's Word. It is for those who yearn for victory through Christ and accept the Bible as God's infallible revelation. In that Word, the PERSON of the devil is as clearly revealed as the PERSON of our Lord Jesus. If we accept its mighty testimony of Christ and heaven, what kind of folly ignores its unveiling of the devil and hell? To question the revelation of Satan is to attack the truth of Christ, for the same Bible declares both — with **equal force!**

When the truths of this book become operative in your life, you will . . .

1. **Have a healthy respect for our adversary.**
2. **Know how he operates.**
3. **Have a defense system for protecting your thought life.**
4. **Be equipped with the spiritual mechanics for resisting him.**

From the bottom of my heart, I believe the Holy Spirit has victory in store for you!

PART ONE

Chapter One

EVERYBODY OUGHT TO KNOW

"For Satan must not be allowed to get the better of us; we know his wiles all too well." (2 Cor. 2:11 NEB)

Art Linkletter's show, "People are Funny," was a TV success. Of all creatures on earth, people are the most fascinating. But there is something curious about Christians. No, not their unshakable faith in an unseen Savior, but their tenacious grasp on the Word of God. Christians insist on the infallibility of the written Word. Challenge its authority or inspiration and they're ready to fight. Seemingly they would die for it.

Here's what's curious. Most Christians deliberately ignore one of the Bible's most cardinal doctrines — **the doctrine of a personal devil.** One hears much about the need for a personal Savior, but the same Bible sets forth a **personal** devil just as clearly and definitely. Don't you find it curious that the truth of Christ can be so widely hearlded, yet the truth of Satan obviously subdued? I find that fact startling, a phenomenon — even supernatural.

Why curious? Listen to the Apostle Paul:

 "Lest Satan should get an advantage of us: for we are not ignorant of his devices" (2 Cor. 2:11 KJV).

OOPS!

Did you catch the "we" in that verse? Can he be serious? Was he referring to the Corinthian church? Satan was shaking that bunch of believers like a rag doll. Perhaps it was true of himself or some with him at Ephesus. BUT what a fantastic overstatement that is today! The average Christian doesn't even know who Satan is, let alone have knowledge of his devices.

What's worse, they smile at the mention of a living, personal devil. One Christian writer has observed:

> "Wonderful is it that he can prevail upon Christian people to banish his name as they do and pastors make only now and then an incidental reference to it in the pulpit . . . while in every room of their households, in every street of our cities, he is incessantly manifesting his hateful presence; perplexing, seducing, embroiling, uprooting, and disorganizing until the whole framework of society is loosened and ready to crumble upon the first shock."*

You don't hear much about Satan today. The church has been willing to relax its hold on the ancient doctrine. Preachers have little to say about him. In some places there is antagonism toward the idea of such a person. Faith in a supernatural Satan has all but collapsed.

---

* Charlotte Elizabeth

17

Say to some Christians, "I wanted to come and see you, but the devil hindered me," mean it, as did the Apostle and watch eyebrows go up. Describe an unsuccessfully treated ailment as "a thorn in the flesh, a messenger of Satan,"* sent to buffet you, and then interpret the looks you get. Try telling your **Christian** employer that a difficulty on the job is due to satanic attack. At once he'll have his doubts about you. Pious smiles may appear to accept what you say about the devil's influence, but behind those smiles your sanity is questioned.

It's not easy to live in a materialistic age where talk of a personal devil is unpopular. Who is willing to speak of him seriously, when such words bring sly glances and looks of suspicion? Who will admit involvement with someone regarded as a figure of speech? It's like believing in Santa Claus. Make more than a joking reference to Satan and people will think you are "a little off." No, it's not easy to get serious about Satan today.

Yet who can read divine prophecy concerning the close of this age and not be obliged to verify every word in the signs about us? Society is throwing off every restraint. The public appetite for sex, violence and a new morality is fed off a large screen in the living room. Politics is a getting game. Alcohol flows like a river. Drugs, teen-age rebellion, riots and the ascending crime rates bespeak an energizing spirit backstage. Satan is organizing the thought life and manipulating the passions of men. Signs indicate a worldwide upheaval calculated to burst forth in a volcano of blasphemy!

---

* 2 Cor. 12:7

Christians may soon be confronted with "all power and signs and lying wonders."* Even now tempting influences are closing in fast. God's people need everything they can get their hands on to live Christ. Few are standing fast in His Name. So many are caught in the "down draft" of this world, there is no recognizable difference between the child of God and the child of the devil.** Being alert to the truth of Satan and equipped to resist him, is a most urgent matter.

Our children sing in Sunday school, "Everybody ought to know . . . Who Jesus is." In view of the swift approach of the evil hour, perhaps we should be teaching them . . .

"EVERYBODY OUGHT TO KNOW
EVERYBODY OUGHT TO KNOW
EVERYBODY OUGHT TO KNOW
WHO SATAN IS!"

SATAN NEEDS DARKNESS

When Herbert Philbrick posed as a Communist for the FBI, his identity had to remain secret. He worked under the cover of aliases. He needed a cloak of **personal darkness** to carry out his mission. The success of his mission depended on it, so did his life. When the truth was revealed years later, the story was captioned, *"I Led Three Lives!"*

The Satan story is similar. One day he will be revealed as he is, but right now his success depends on personal darkness — absolute obscurity — and he's getting it. By means of supernatural resources, he has been able to throw a cover of ignorance over the body of Christ. The way he rules mankind, **practically unnoticed**, is a fascinating mystery.

---

* 2 Thess. 2:9 ** 1 John 3:10

If Satan's success depends on secrecy and darkness, then turning on the light to expose him can hurt his operation. Just as publicity would haved ruined Herbert Philbrick as an undercover agent, so can exposure cancel much of Satan's power. Therefore, such an exposure is our beginning point. The first thing Christians need to know about Satan is **WHO** HE IS.

THE FUND OF KNOWLEDGE

When I discovered Satan alive and tasted the thrill of having him flee, I knew it was to be shared with God's people. Before writing, I checked to see what was already available on the subject. There is no point in reproducing truths already in print. I began reading every book and article I could find. There is a useful store of knowledge scattered throughout books published in the last 75 years.

In more than 60 volumes, I found a body of agreed truth. Enough to satisfy me that the Holy Spirit already has a FUND OF KNOWLEDGE on deposit for the church. There is a concensus among writers like Chafer, Unger, Lewis, Koch, Morgan, Jennings and the Catholic fathers (amazingly on target), which provides a springboard from which to launch an exposition. I will list some facts below, which if we can accept them, will give us a basis for moving on to things not a part of any writings.

❶ SATAN, A CREATED BEING

Most expositors agree that the passages of Isa. 14 and Ezek. 28 look beyond the Kings of Tyre and Babylon and are detailed descriptions of the person of Satan. Ormiston and Jennings open these verses in lovely detail.

a. Satan was created by the Lord Jesus (Col. 1:16). Heaven's skill and love went into making him after the divine image. He was vested with every grace and anointed as the guardian of God's glory. Probably the Savior and Satan were close, personal friends in those days. In heaven, Satan was the delight of the Lord and at home in the presence of God. He wore righteousness comfortably. He was holiness personified.

b. Satan seems to have been given the task of producing a race of citizens for heaven. He was to lead them in open praise and adoration of the Most High. He was absolutely perfect in every way, with his glory second only to that of God. He was the best God could create. None was wiser, more beautiful, or more important. And like his Creator, he was FREE.

c. It is not certain WHERE Satan was producing the race of citizens; whether in heaven itself or on the earth. The chaos of Gen. 1:2 may indicate a ruin of the earth occurred prior to the (re)creation account of Genesis 1:3. Some hold that Satan's kingdom was here. Others hold that he merely destroyed the universes in rage after his revolt was thwarted. In any event, it is clear he wanted this world when creation was completed and given to Adam.

❷ SATAN'S SIN

a. Made like his Creator, completely free to exercise his will, Satan could do or not do the will of God as he saw fit. He had the power to revolt if he wanted to. He was not expected to covet his Maker's throne, for he seemingly held every honor but that. Ezekiel indicates he lived to praise God. But alas, the day came when "INIQUITY WAS FOUND" in him. The reason for that remains locked with God, for the time. If sin can be defined as rebellion against the known will of God, sin began that day.

b. Satan's rebellion was occasioned by self-deception. He was enamoured with his own beauty, impressed with his wisdom, and exalted by the importance of his job. Though a created being, he deluded himself into thinking he could be "like the Most High." The blinding power of self-affection is manifested when a created being thinks to replace his Creator.

c. Satan's FREEWILL decision to exalt himself against God was his sin. Pride was the energizing factor. Satan, second in command to God Himself, had great forces under him. Already accustomed to his leadership, it wasn't too hard to involve many of them in the rebellion. They are the "principalities and powers" referred to by Paul, for they retain their rank and dignity, as does Satan. Those who participated are called, "fallen angels" or "demons." Those who refused are called the "angels of God."

❸ SATAN FALLEN

a. Satan's rebellion cost him his job and brought eternal banishment from the kingdom of God. An ETERNAL being, like his Creator, he would spend eternity some place other than in heaven. Hell was "created for the devil and his angels" before the program of "man on the earth" was started. Though fallen, he still retains all that God built into him. He is still mighty.

b. Instead of casting Satan directly into hell, God would SALVAGE something from the huge investment. The God of Romans 8:28 would take what was invested in Satan and use it for His glory. He would still accomplish His first intention. Now that sin was available, He would EXPLOIT it. Instead of discarding Satan, his great powers would be used to provide a competitive god, making possible a genuine test for man's affection. Sin would be useful in developing a race of TESTED citizens. It wasn't available until Satan's fall.

c. Satan's greatness is now perverted. His wisdom is turned to guile and deceit. His tremendous intelligence produces craftiness and treachery. His fantastic genius has turned from bringing glory to God, to gratifying himself. His former dwelling in holiness gives him a knowledge of both "good and evil." Thoroughly schooled in righteousness, he now plumbs the depths of wickedness. Once a peer of holiness, he is now a personification of evil. He is able to make evil look good and good look evil, since he has lived on "BOTH SIDES OF THE TRACKS."

d. Satan is over-qualified to tempt man. He operates in the spirit. He has at least 7000 years experience in dealing with human weakness. He can give temporal rewards to those who serve him. He has lost none of his powers, retaining even his rank. He is the supreme being of the evil world. His great wisdom makes it easy for him to deceive and delude those not illumined by God's Word. He can distort truth so masterfully even those who desire to live for Christ are easily manipulated even when they "watch and pray."

❹ GOD OF THIS WORLD

a. Adam was placed on the earth with authority over it. He was told to subdue it and exercise dominion over everything that moved (Gen. 1:28). When Adam was tested, he knew clearly what was involved.

The test began in a beautiful garden with Adam's wife, Eve (what better way to get to a man?). The serpent spoke, "Yea, hath God said, ye shall not eat of every tree of the garden?" (Gen. 3:1). Poor Eve. She couldn't know what was taking place. No one had told her about a personal devil.

Did that innocent girl suspect a gallery of powers, an audience of spirit beings, was listening to her conversa-

23

tion with Satan? She didn't know a world of danger hovered **unseen.**

Were not her sight limited to the eyes that came with her body, she could have beheld a multitude of spiritual dignitaries holding their breath. A great host watched. Satan was demonstrating how easy it is to trick people. The spirit world was getting a training lesson.

Doubtless Eve talked with this beautiful pet before. It had the power of speech, likely surpassing that of the minah bird or parakeet. This day was different. Ordered speech was coming out. The animal was presenting the most noble thing a man can consider — **being like God.**

Had she looked closer, she might have beheld the devilish glint in the serpent's eye. No longer was this a marvellous creature of the field speaking, but a cardinal of Heaven. The disguise was perfect. Eve was impressed. The Generalissimo of Evil was at work. And his forces were ready to pounce on the world as soon as he made the kill.

Much was at stake. If Satan could get this first pair, he would get the world. The divine plan called for children to be born of their parents. This was how the earth was to be filled. If Satan could get the first parents, he would inherit their offspring. If Eve would fall for Satan's suggestion, the human race would become the devil's property. .

It was a critical moment. The spirit world poised in breathless anticipation. Then it happened! Eve did eat. And she gave it to Adam. Satan got Adam without a word. The natural force of family devotion captured him without a shot. He was not deceived (1 Tim. 2:14). By a single act, he joined the rebel gang. And since that gang already had a chief, Adam forfeited his position as ruler of the world. When Adam disobeyed, the control

24

of mankind passed to Satan. He is the king of the disobeyers. When the first man forfeited his dominion, Satan became "god of this world" (2 Cor. 4:4). He was already a god. Adam's rebellion simply gave him control of the world.

Successful in deceiving Eve, Satan then used Adam's affection for her to draw the first man into his coils. God had actually given the entire world into Adam's hands. So the devil, in tricking him out of it, LEGALLY ACQUIRED THE WORLD and all of mankind.

b. The fall of Adam and the fall of Satan were identical. Both exalted their sovereign wills against the known will of God. The fall of Adam was no surprise. A redemption plan had already been devised, "from the foundation of the world."

c. No sooner did Adam fall than it was announced Satan had an enemy mightier than he. Satan was to meet defeat at the hands of the Seed of the woman. This Seed, it was promised, would "bruise thy head" (Gen. 3:15). Satan's newly gained kingdom was threatened by a Person Who would arrive in the world via the birth process. This accounts for Satan's slaughter of the infants when he found Herod a cooperative tool. It also led Satan to think that physical death could destroy Christ.

d. Satan exercises his control over fallen man by virtue of his dominion over all disobeyers. It is written, "All have sinned" (Rom. 3:23), thus all join the gang of which Satan is head. There is no escape from the dominion apart from outside help.

e. Satan is the author of all evil, sickness and suffering in this present world. He has a hand in the viciousness of the animal kingdom, the pestilence, floods, vegetable blight and tragedy. God uses all these things, even as He uses Satan, to provide the stresses needed to bring His sons to maturity.

❺ SATAN'S BLUNDER

a. Satan goofed when he engineered the death of the Lord Jesus. He didn't dream that Christ's obedience unto death (Phil. 2:8) would provide a righteousness which could release people from satanic control. He thought he was getting rid of his enemy when Jesus died. Too late he discovered it was an ingenious "escape hatch" out of his kingdom (1 Cor. 2:7, 8).

26

When Jesus said, **"It is accomplished,"** Satan's fate was sealed and the way was opened for mankind to be placed into the kingdom of God (Col. 1:13,14).

b. When the Lord Jesus rose from the grave, it was demonstrated that man, "born of a woman," does not die. He "brought life and immortality to light" (2 Tim. 1:10). Men could now see that physical death is harmless and life persists after the body ceases to function. The fear of death had been one of Satan's prime tools in prompting men to get all they could while the getting was good. But if life endures after physical death, God's promises take on a new look. Lazarus' experience further certified death's harmlessness. Satan apparently disbelieved or discounted the resurrection plans.

c. Satan's fate was sealed that day. The Cross heralded the end of his kingdom. His days were numbered. If he had any doubts about that, he could read it in the Scriptures for himself. The prophecies dealing with his fate would stand, now that the Son of God validated the Word of God by His resurrection. In the time remaining, Satan takes out his bitterness on mankind. He lives to hurt, with the children of God special objects of his ha-

27

tred. His way of retaliating against the Lord is laying waste to the lives of God's people. He prosecutes every opportunity with determination. He knows any loss suffered by Christians in this life is eternal.

d. Satan's rage mounts as his end approaches. His fury will be greatest when he is cast from the spirit world (Rev. 12). He will then be forced to occupy a physical body stripped of his unseen ability to reach and influence the minds of men. He will indwell the body of his selected world ruler and offer himself to mankind as the true God. He will sit in the temple posing as the Most High (2 Thess. 2:4), something he coveted from the beginning. His reign will be brief, terminated by the personal appearance of the Lord Jesus . . .

 ". . . whom the Lord shall consume with the Spirit of His mouth, and shall destroy with the brightness of His coming" (2 Thess. 2:8 KJV).*

❻ SATAN'S LIMITATIONS

a. Inasmuch as Satan blundered by executing the Lord Jesus, it is safe to say he does not have all-knowledge. Paul mentions a hidden wisdom "Which none of the princes of this world knew: for had they known it, they would not have crucified the Lord of glory" (1 Cor. 2:8). It is certain that Satan knows not the "day nor the hour" of final revelation. Not even the Son was permitted to know that (Matt. 24:36).

b. Most authors state that Satan is not omnipresent. Yet all agree he has access to people, either directly or indirectly. No one seems to be beyond his reach. However he is not allowed to make direct attacks upon human bodies, except as he is permitted to engineer

*For detailed study of Satan's activities in the end time, consult the author's book **LATEST WORD ON THE LAST DAYS.**

circumstances. Those also must be severely limited, since he could use the freeways to get rid of many of us. His blows against our bodies appear to be limited to the power of suggestion and the resulting psychosomatic disorders. When GIVEN PERMISSION by any individual, he is able to possess that person in both mind and body.

c. He is therefore not omnipotent. Obviously he cannot take lives at will otherwise we'd all be dead. Since Christians are the "salt of the earth," he has good reason to wipe them out. He would if he could. He seems to have power over the elements, vis., the storm on the sea of Galilee which Jesus rebuked. Destruction is written everywhere in the universe. Death is everywhere. Even bugs, weeds, deadly creatures, and floods appear to be under satanic control. God is hardly the author of the fantastic struggle to survive found in the world.

d. Satan's contact with the believer is through the OLD NATURE only. He has no access to the NEW NATURE received at salvation. The Christian is ALWAYS FREE to choose between his two natures. Thus Satan cannot touch the WILL of the believer. Consequently any CONTROL over the Christian is by permission or individual surrender to him. His influence is limited to the intellectual and emotional pressures he can exert via the old nature. Please keep this fact in mind as you read the book.

If we can agree to this rather sketchy list of facts about Satan, or most of them, we will have a common basis for our focus on his attacks against God's people. Studies in the background are fascinating. I revel in all the good things available. But these ideas, selected from the FUND OF KNOWLEDGE will get us started.

REVELATION A PRIME TOOL

There are limits on human knowledge. It is easy to roam amid foolish speculation. We must avoid that.

However, the probings of an illumined imagination are never a hindrance. Something else is, though — **skepticism**. This is the biggest hurdle for a serious discussion of Satan.

Inasmuch as the devil and his legions move about **unseen**, the blackout today isn't hard to understand. People are reluctant to take the unseen world seriously. It isn't natural to do so, of course — it's supernatural. That's a bad word, too. It is not sophisticated to probe a sphere where scientific methods and deductions produce nothing. Revelation is not always regarded as a respectable tool.

Yet, inspiration is clearly a Scriptural tool:

 "Through the Spirit, however, God has revealed it to us; for the Spirit fathoms everything, even the deep things of God. And we have received, not the spirit of the world but the Spirit that comes from God, in order that we may know the things which God has freely given us" (1 Cor. 2:10, 12 MLB).

Revelation by the Holy Spirit is one of our prime tools. Do we not learn as HE illumines our personal experiences by the Word of God? No Christian should be afraid of trusting the Spirit of God as a teacher, for HE is also our guarantee from error.*

If I write by the Spirit of God, then you may test what you read by the same Spirit. If, through the weakness of the flesh, I err, you can determine which things carry His witness to your heart. We live in a time when false spirits are surging and it is incumbent upon God's people to exercise discernment. You should try by God's Word and His Spirit what you

---

*1John 4:1, 1 John 2:27

read here. If my words help you to live closer to the Lord Jesus and exalt Him, then you can accept them. If you find they hinder your relationship or dilute your victory in any way, you should discard them.

But do not be afraid to trust the leadership of the Spirit of God in these things. For people who believe only in what they can see, even faith in God is not respectable. Think what their reaction would be to the idea of a personal devil! We cannot let ourselves be influenced by them. God's Word is clear in this matter. If we take it seriously, we will put the scoffers behind us.

THE WEIGHT OF THE WORD

To treasure the Word of God and remain indifferent to the massive revelation of the devil is not wise. A wealth of Bible material unveils Satan, demons and supernaturalism. The number of passages which could be expounded is tremendous. They combine to give a very comprehensive picture of our enemy.

Not only is the PERSON of Satan set forth clearly, but his WORKING is as fully manifested as that of the Holy Spirit. If Christians find what God has to say about His Spirit no test of reason, they should find it no more difficult to believe what is said about Satan. It takes the same faith to discern him as it does the Spirit of God. The ministry of one is no harder to imagine than the other. With that, note Paul's assertion that a state of war exists:

"For our struggle is not against flesh and blood, but against rulers, against powers, against the world forces of this darkness, against the spiritual forces of wickedness in the heavenly places" (Eph. 6:12 NAS).

Look at that! Who can miss the contest! It doesn't take a dean of expositors to see the majestic lineup of

31

evil princes here. Is not a host of unseen powers arrayed against God's people? How can this be taken lightly? The Christian who fails to consider the implications of such a thing is a fool. To ignore that the HEAD of this evil army is his **personal** enemy is blindness. The worst kind. For it is not accidental blindness, but **deliberate.**

Does anyone have to tell you this is spiritual war? The fact of "heavenly places" removes any thought of physical encounters with these people. The battlefield is in the spirit, beyond the pale of the flesh. But that doesn't make it vague or unreal. God's Word beams much light on activities in the spirit, as any serious Bible student knows.

For example, a knowledge of the workings of the Holy Spirit also tells a great deal about Satan. Since he is a counterfeiter, we can be certain he is copying, (if not using precisely) the same techniques as the Spirit of God. May not the degree to which a reader understands the workings of the Holy Spirit, be the degree to which he can comprehend the methods of the **unholy spirit?** Why not?

- **Both people are spirit beings**
- **Both operate in the spirit**
- **Both deal directly with man**
- **Both want the same thing from man**

As we move along in our probe, the weight of Scripture will show this to be clearly so.

FORGET DEMONOLOGY

This is not a book on demonology.

It has to do with Satan and deals with him as our unique enemy. I want you to **forget about demons** for the time. Does not Satan have legions of fallen angels to do his bidding? Yes. Hosts of evil spirits (demons, if you prefer) carry out his orders. But I am satisfied their role is **minor** and that their work is IN ADDITION TO HIS.

I am satisfied that demons no more do the work of Satan, than the angels of God do the work of the Holy Spirit. Satan's subordinates hold and maintain his conquests, but he is the conqueror. He is the attacker. As the Holy Spirit is the One Who brings the conviction of sin, certifies the Word of God and makes Christ real to individuals, so also does the **unholy spirit** personally lead, tempt and inspire men to do evil. Demons should no more be mentioned in this regard than angels can be said to establish the indwelling presence of Christ.

The work of God's angels is defined:

 "Are they not all ministering spirits, sent out to render service for the sake of those who will inherit salvation?" (Heb. 1:14 NAS).

It is the Holy Spirit, **Himself,** Who forms Christ in us and Who "bears witness with our spirit that we are children of God" (Rom. 8:16 NAS). This is no tiny distinction. The difference between the work of the Holy Spirit and God's angels is like night and day. So it is with Satan and the angels serving him.

Almost every book on the subject emphasizes the afflicting presence of demons. Satan is no fool. He'll leak out information on demons so as to distract writers and investigators. Since demons do cause physical disorders, they earn a lot of attention. People get excited when their bodies are hurt. Demon studies are popular because they **hint** a promise of healing. And you know the extent to which people will go for healing. Right now I know a man who drives hundreds of miles to Mexico for cancer treatments because the drug used there is outlawed in this country.

Satan has used demonology as a smoke screen to divert attention from himself. If writers can be shifted to his **underlings,** he continues to enjoy the blackout he needs. And readers are easily engrossed where the physical body is concerned. Until more light is given me, I insist their role is minor by comparison. He is the **source** of our affliction. Christian psychology is turning up more on demon activity every day, while the **prince** of demons is being ignored.

In my opinion, demonology is best left as a separate study while we **turn the spotlight** on Satan. He is our enemy and demons can do nothing apart from him. If we learn how to deal with him, we have little to fear from demons. So put them out of your mind as you read this book. Think only in terms of our one vicious enemy — **Satan.** Think of him as your **personal** adversary whose working is akin to that of the Holy Spirit. If you find yourself wondering about demons, then think of them as being to Satan what the angels of God are to the Holy Spirit.

Satan's kingdom is large. It takes an enormous chain of command to operate it. The hierarchy of beings cited by Paul is needed to maintain it. But there is only **one** devil. He was Jesus' **singular** enemy. He is your enemy right now.

YOUR PERSONAL DEVIL

That's how I want you to think of Satan. I want you to put him in the same category as the Lord Jesus — as far as **importance** is concerned. Does that shock you? Here's why I say that. Just as you dealt with the Person of Jesus for salvation, so must you deal with the **person** of Satan for victory. If we ignore Jesus, there is no salvation. If we ignore Satan, there can be no full victory. See it like this:

★ Salvation requires a PERSONAL Savior!
★ Victory requires a PERSONAL enemy!

But let me be clear. All victory is **through** our Lord Jesus Christ. Yet victory itself means a fight and a fight requires an enemy. Therefore every victory you have ever enjoyed in the Christian life has meant some kind of a defeat for Satan. No, you were not conscious of the devil. Nonetheless your victory handed him a defeat. There can be no forward step in faith without some kind of a blow against Satan. If all of your dealings with Satan have been unknowing and unwitting, think what your progress in Christ could be if you began to deal with the enemy **knowingly.** Think what might happen in your life if you became as serious in dealing with Satan for victory as you deal with Jesus for salvation!

I am asking you to concentrate on two people. The Holy Spirit and the unholy spirit. See both of them as:

1. **Present with you**
2. **Giving you personal attention**
3. **Possessed of fantastic powers in the spirit world**
4. **Ready to exercise whatever dominion you will permit**

Yes, you have a free will. You are responsible for which spirit exercises the most influence over your thoughts and actions. That's what makes this a subtle business. If the unholy spirit can get you to do his will, you do so of your **own free choice.** Subsequently you are judged for it, because your choice is deliberate.

● After you finish the book, you can test these truths to see whether they hinder or help your life in Christ. For the time being, put them with other truths you will pick up and reserve judgment until you can make the proper tests. The "proof of the pudding is in the eating," and the test of these things is what they do for you in your life.

This chapter began stating that Christians are funny, because they ignore one of the most vital doctrines of the Book they cherish. If this manual does what it is supposed to, you will still be a funny Christian. Not because you ignore the Word you treasure, but because you live in a day when it is funny to believe in a **personal devil.**

HAPPENING TO YOU?

If you're honest with yourself, you'll agree you are nowhere near what you ought to be in Christ. Don't you want to be a better Christian than you are right now? Sure. Without realizing it, your personal adversary, the devil, is directing your life. His subtle wisdom, his ingenious devices, make it easy for him to manipulate you. An outsider maneuvers you in such a way you neither suspect it or notice it. Everything you do and say **appears to be** your own idea, but is isn't.

Satan can make you forget Jesus hours on end. He can cause you to sit for an entire evening in front of the TV filling your mind with worthless trivia.

If you think no one is that clever, you're mistaken. Satan is. He can get you to waste one day after another. He can cause you to forget Jesus hours upon end. He can make you misbehave and think you're not so bad. He can plant evil thoughts in your mind and you'll think you're clean in God's sight. He can cause you to be idle and think you're making progress in Christ. That's why I say no Christian is a match for him. The average Christian doesn't dream that his life is being led by Satan. He doesn't suspect the power that is exercised over him. He may laugh at poor Eve, but he is no better off!

Most Christians can look back a year to see little or no change. They are still the same persons. Their personalities are no sweeter, the dedication of their talents is stabilized, their pocketbooks are just as tight and their occupation with the world is as solidly fixed. There's no increase in surrender, devotion or service. They go year after year without much change.

Do Christians want this? No. Yet it happens. Why? If you haven't begun to suspect a mighty adversary is dedicated to keep you from living Christ, you will when you see how he works. That's next.

Chapter Two

TO CAPTURE
A MAN!

---

*"and they may come to their senses and escape from
the snare of the devil, having been held captive by
him to do his will"* (2 Tim. 2:26 NAS).

Drs. William Culbertson and Irwin Moon, of Moody
Bible Institute, landed their private plane in a small
African country to visit a mission station. The next
morning they arrived at the airstrip to find it surround-
ed by barbed wire and machine guns. During the night
Communists had seized power by taking control of the
radio stations and transportation facilities. Only quick
Yankee diplomacy allowed the brethren to get away
safely.

A tiny nation went to bed free and awakened the next morning under Communist control. Yet the Communists know that military force does not really capture men. The Berlin wall, for example, may restrict travel, but it does not make Communists of people. The only way to capture a man is to get him to think like you do. Ideas capture men, not weapons.

Win a man's mind and you have him. Capture his thoughts and you control him. Does not the wisdom of the Holy Spirit say:

"For as he thinketh in his heart, so is he . . ."
(Prov. 23:7 KJV).

If you can find a way to get your ideas inside another, so that he thinks as you do, you gain that man. Man is the product of his thinking. Why else do Communists brainwash their prisoners? It explains, too, their passion for propaganda. They flood the world with their literature.

SATAN WANTS MEN'S MINDS

The Apostle feared Satan as the attacker of our minds:

"But I am afraid, lest as the serpent deceived Eve by his craftiness, your minds should be led astray from the simplicity and purity of devotion to Christ" (2 Cor. 11:3 NAS).

That's clear enough. Paul knew of Satan's crafty ability to lead Christians from the pure devotion to Jesus. All the evil one need do is reach our minds with his corruptive suggestions and we bend to his will. The subtlety which beguiled Eve is just as mighty today. The devil manipulates the minds of God's people with surprising ease.

● Ever wonder why you cannot remember Scripture passages as you would like? Or why your mind wanders at prayer time? And when you are in prayer-fellowship with others you find it difficult to remain in focus with them? Satan is responsible. Christians have badly underestimated him at this point.

The undisciplined mind is wide open to satanic attack. If you do not consciously control **every thought** going through your head (and who does?), the resulting slackness makes it easy for Satan to introduce his own ideas. You are not aware that he does this, for the thoughts appear as your own. You say to me, "How can I control every thought?" I answer, "If you don't, a mastermind is ready to." If we are careless about God's Word, (AS WE THINK IN OUR HEARTS, SO ARE WE), Satan isn't. He counts on it and puts it to work for him. An undisciplined thought life makes one vulnerable to the devil. It takes very little to get a man to think as Satan does.

If you think I am unreasonable to suggest the **complete** discipline of your mind, the Apostle Paul is even more definite:

 "For the weapons of our warfare are not carnal, but mighty through God to the pulling down of strongholds; casting down imaginations and every high thing that exalteth itself against the knowledge of God, and bringing into captivity EVERY THOUGHT to the obedience of Christ!" (2 Cor. 10:4,5 KJV).

Notice, "every thought." Thinking is a contest. If you don't believe that, try keeping your mind on Jesus for

40

five minutes solid. You'll find a state of war exists — a thought war:

 "**For we wrestle not against flesh and blood, but against principalities, against powers, against the rulers of the darkness of this world, against spiritual wickedness in high places**" (Eph. 6:12 KJV).

Evil strongholds are maintained for the purpose of clouding our minds. Spiritual forces are arrayed to keep us from occupying with Christ. Dignitaries make it their business to keep us from setting our "affection on things above" (Col. 3:2). The resources of spiritual wickedness are organized to make us forget Jesus most of the day. So again, try "bringing into captivity every thought to the obedience of Christ," and see if it doesn't amount to a military campaign!

The Holy Spirit warns of mental weariness in devoting ourselves to Jesus:

 "**For consider Him that endured such contradiction of sinners against Himself, lest ye be wearied and FAINT IN YOUR MINDS**" (Heb. 12:3 KJV).

See the battlefield? It's the thought life of the Christian. Spiritual war is real. Look at the equipment the Apostle cites as Christian armor. Observe that it is all mental preparation.

If Satan's lordship over humanity is maintained by his control of our thought life, Christian victory surely rests in the area of the disciplined mind. "Let this MIND be in you, which was also in Christ Jesus" (Phil. 2:5) is thought-war strategy.

Thus, the mind of man is the theatre of satanic operation. The extent to which he can influence the thoughts of people is the extent to which he can control them. In fact, he must work with the human mind, for he has nothing else. That may surprise you. You say, "Doesn't he attack men's bodies?" Ah, but only as the author of PSYCHOSOMATIC DISORDERS. Doctors quickly allow that 65%-85% of the cases coming to them show no pathology (tissue disease). The huge bulk of body afflictions originate in the human mind, not in the members.

You've read enough articles in **Reader's Digest** to know what I am talking about. A person's mind seriously affects his body. The public is fast becoming aware that most ailments are neuro-psychic in origin.*

SATAN'S PERSONAL ATTACK

To be a **personal** adversary, Satan has to be present to each Christian. This raises a theological question. Is Satan OMNIPRESENT? That is, can he be EVERY PLACE at once? If he is to be present to every Christian, he has to be in more than one place at a time. We need to discuss his ability to press a full scale attack **personally** against every child of God.

The Scriptures fit when Satan is viewed as a present spirit, who deals **personally** with individuals:

> **"But if our Gospel be hid, it is hid to them that are lost: in whom the GOD OF THIS WORLD HATH BLINDED THE MINDS of them which believe not . . ."** (2 Cor. 4:3, 4 KJV).

> **"But RESIST HIM, firm in your faith, knowing that the same experiences of suffering are being accomplished by your brethren who are in the world"** (1 Peter 5:9 NAS).

---

*See chapter five "How Your Mind Affects Your Body" in the author's book JESUS WANTS YOU WELL!

42

That sounds **personal** to me.

I have read discussions as to how underlings could do this for Satan, but the constructions seem more forced than seeing Satan as doing it himself. The text of our book says . . .

"Resist the devil (not demons) and he (not they) will flee from you!" (James 4:7)

If man can do it . . . ?

In our day the idea of PRESENCE is not so formidable. Not since the advent of television. As I write these lines, more than 400 million people are watching by satellite the World Cup Soccer matches being held in West Germany. Since the tournament began, more than 2 billion people have enjoyed the game as though they were right there. The people saw the action as it happened. They became involved in the plays and were caught up in the thrill as they took place.

This modern miracle helps us understand how Satan can simulate the working of the Holy Spirit to bring his presence to each life. Most adults have a rough idea how it works.

In the case of the soccer match, the camera on the field transmits the electronic signal to the main studio. The studio broadcasts it up to the 3 communication satellites which receive the signal from earth, amplify it, and transmit it to other points on earth. The 3 satellite locations above the earth's equator can provide complete coverage of the earth's surface.

The earth station receives the satellite transmission, and using a carrier wave, feeds it to an antenna which broadcasts it over a large region. The waves are sensed by antennas connected to TV receivers and displayed on the screen. The very same picture that appears on TV in the home is a duplicate of the one on the field. There is **no limit** to the number of sets which can tune to that station and get the same picture.

Therefore, if men can design TV equipment to bring the presence of personalities into our homes all over the earth, surely Satan, with all his **spiritual** resources, can bring his presence to all of our lives. Don't you think it would be easier for him as the "prince of the power of the air," to do this in the **spirit world,** than for men with carrier waves and satellites in the physical world? To insist that Satan cannot be in more than one place at a time is to place a limitation on him being out-paced BY MEN THEMSELVES.

Television may be a clumsy human illustration, but it helps us to understand Satan's presence. If finite men can **infinitely** reproduce their presence in homes, how much **easier** must it be for the "god of this world," to bring his presence to you and me? I feel it is risky to assume our enemy is anything but PRESENT. Please note that I have not said that he was omnipresent. Only that he is present.

SCRIPTURAL INDICATIONS

When the Apostle Paul declares Satan to be "god of this world," he awards him **theological** authority. When Jesus calls him the "prince of this world," He ascribes

44

him **political** authority over mankind.* But when Paul dubs him, "the prince of the power of the air," it is a description of his **spiritual dominion** as the unholy spirit, his power to do a work **inside** people. Listen:

". . . in time past ye walked according to the course of this world, according to the prince of the power of the air, the spirit that now worketh in the children of disobedience . . ." (Eph. 2:2 KJV).

Disregard for a moment that this refers to the unsaved. Instead see how Satan governs mankind as the **unholy spirit**. What kind of prince can do this? Here is a fantastic mastery of free souls. The "prince of the power of the air" WORKETH INSIDE PEOPLE. The force of the passage rests on that word, "**worketh.**" And it is identical to the one used where God's indwelling is stated:

"For it is God which WORKETH in you both to will and to do of HIS good pleasure" (Phil. 2:13 KJV).

Satan works in people the same way. I see no difference in the way the God of Heaven and the god of this world reach and carry out their respective ambitions in the hearts of men.

"But all these (gifts) WORKETH that One and Selfsame Spirit, dividing to every man severally as He will" (1 Cor. 12:11 KJV).

Satan does the same. By his spirit (his presence actually), he "worketh" in people so that they will walk according to his will. Satan works out his will in men just as God works out His will in those who will let Him.

---
*John 12:31, 14:30, 16:11

Now don't be offended that I use what you know of the Holy Spirit's operation to explain the devil's ability to influence and maneuver people after his will. He is a god. He operates in the spirit. He beholds all that the Spirit of God does in us and has the ability to counterfeit, if not duplicate it. Always to serve his evil purposes, of course.

It is my conviction concerning Satan's presence that makes me respect him as my **personal** enemy.

HOW SATAN SEES

 "Nothing in all creation is hidden from God's sight. Everything is uncovered and laid bare before the eyes of Him to Whom we must give account" (Heb. 4:13 NIV).

That passage speaks of God's all-seeing eye. But the same thing can be said of the "god of this world." The other ruler of mankind doesn't miss anything either. Consider how hearts are exposed to his evil gaze:

 "When anyone hears the message of the kingdom and does not understand it, the evil one comes and snatches away what is sown in his heart . . ." (Matt. 13:19 MLB).

Can you picture what it takes to do that? Not only does the wicked one have to be present, but he has to know what is going on IN THE UNDERSTANDING of the listener! See those words, **"DOES NOT UNDERSTAND IT?"** Where does a person have to stand to behold the reasonings of another? What ability is required to do this? Why, the heart and mind of the reasoner must be exposed to Satan's view. How does Satan know that someone doesn't understand the Gospel unless he beholds the very thoughts. He has to see them! That means the whole mental experience is laid bare befor him.

Then see that this is only PART of Satan's ability. On top of that he has the power to SNATCH THE TRUTH AWAY! Jesus says so. He can take the Word of God right out of a man's heart. Sure you want to know how he does it, that comes later. Right now don't miss the wonder of what our Lord has said. Then there's something worse to consider:

 "Then Peter said, 'Ananias, how is it that Satan has so FILLED YOUR HEART that you have lied to the Holy Spirit . . .?' " (Acts 5:3 NIV).

Look at these amazing feats of Satan!

1. He has to be present to see the inner workings of the mind.
2. The thought life is laid open to his inspection.
3. He has the power to take away the Word of God.
4. He can introduce his own ideas.

Few suspect the real power of the enemy. And don't miss the fact that our Lord Jesus said . . . "When ANYONE," not the unsaved. Anyone. Consider also, that none of this could be done if Satan were not present to our thought life.

WAR CENTER

Clearly the center of our warfare is our mind. If Satan can keep Christians from storing God's Word, their prime weapon against him is gone. If he can cause a mind to flit among the trash and trivia of our day, it will be useless to the Holy Spirit. Since he has the power to introduce ideas, mental wandering is accomplished easily. The mind, also the channel for the Spirit of God, is quickly blocked with foolish imaginations and notions.

47

Can we understand Peter's concern now? "Gird up the loins of your mind," he says (1 Peter 1:13). And why? It has to be ready to move fast. An adversary lurks who can plant ideas faster than an arrow leaves the bow. So, **"Be sober,"** he warns, **"be vigilant; because your adversary the devil, as a roaring lion, walketh about, seeking whom he may devour"** (1 Peter 5:8 KJV).*

He blinds the minds of the unsaved and leads them to substitute gods of their own manufacturing in place of the true God. He leads Christians to occupy with physical things to the neglect of the Lord Jesus. Occupation with this world renders them useless for Gospel obedience, forfeits their future rewards and blinds them to the swift approach of the day of accounting. Doubt that he has such power? Then ask yourself:

1. **Do I come anywhere near being what I ought to be for Christ?**
2. **How far am I from bringing every thought into captivity for Christ?**
3. **Does making a living and providing for my family concern me more than laying up treasure in heaven?**
4. **Is what I do and say carefully weighed in the light of the judgment seat of Christ?**
5. **Do I consciously work at preparing myself to live with a Holy God?**

---

* . . ."As a roaring lion." This metaphorical expression of the spirit must not be taken as teaching Satan makes a loud declaration of his fiendish purposes when he seeks his prey. The steps of a lion are soft and stealthy. His terrible 'roar' is uttered only when his prey is secured. Usually it is as he is about to seize it. Burder's Oriental Customs, Vol. ii, p. 432; and Berchart, Vol. ii, p. 729.

6. Do I live as though my future state depends on my faithful stewardship of this life?
7. What have I deliberately done today to make myself more like Christ?

Your answers to these questions will give you an idea of how much control Satan has over your mind.

THREE TENSES OF SALVATION

A Salvation Army lass stopped a noted clergyman on the street.

"Sir," she challenged, "Are you saved?" His reply caught her off guard.

"Indeed I am, sometimes, but not yet!" She couldn't let that go by.

"What kind of an answer is that?" She retorted.

"Well, if you mean am I saved from the **guilt** of sin, indeed I am. If you mean am I saved from the **power** of sin, I can only say, sometimes. If you mean am I saved from the **presence** of sin, then definitely not!"

This clergyman displayed sound theology. He was referring to the three tenses of salvation. One tense, as you know, looks back to the cross where the GUILT of sin was cared for. Another tense looks down where our feet stand right now and has to do with the POWER of sin in our daily lives. The third tense looks forward to the time when we will be delivered from the PRESENCE of sin.

The subject of salvation can never be treated correctly without distinguishing between these three tenses:

49

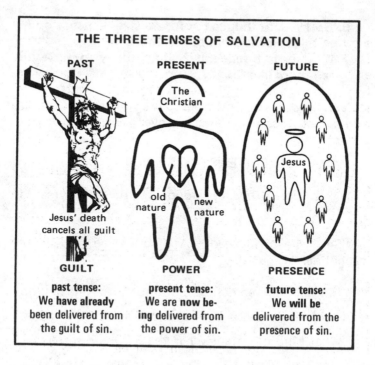

THE THREE TENSES OF SALVATION

PAST — PRESENT — FUTURE

The Christian

old nature | new nature

Jesus

Jesus' death cancels all guilt

GUILT — POWER — PRESENCE

past tense:
We **have already** been delivered from the guilt of sin.

present tense:
We are **now** being delivered from the power of sin.

future tense:
We **will be** delivered from the presence of sin.

● The past is settled. There is nothing Satan can do about the GUILT of sin in the life of a Christian. Nothing could be truer than the song, *"Jesus paid it all!"* That sings out the glad news that Jesus bore our **guilt** for sin. It is sin's GUILT that sends men to hell. The word "guilty" brings the penalty. Usually when Christians speak of a man as being saved, they are referring to the past tense. He has been delivered from the **guilt** of sin. No one can touch that.

● The present tense of salvation is something else. The **power** of sin lingers. When a man receives Christ, he receives a righteous nature. But this is in addition to the OLD nature which he already had, a nature prone to do evil. Once he tries to live a godly life, he finds the war between his two natures almost forbids it. As a result he sins many times. It is then that he discovers the POWER of sin in his life. This is Satan's strength against us.

50

You say, "Are we not forgiven?" Yes, sin will not send us to hell, but that doesn't kill a man's appetite for evil. There is a propensity, a bent, a tendency to do evil that is woven into the warp and woof of humanity. It is the yearning for sin, embedded in the structure of society, that gives Satan his power. Without that, he would be impotent. His suggestions would then fall on deaf ears.

Sinful man likes sin. Satanic suggestions catering to man's sinful desires find ready acceptance. Temptation is legitimate because men have appetites which can be enticed. If men hated sin, Satan would have no power at all. It is the fact of sinful desires residing in our members that makes temptation possible.

● Then there's the future tense of salvation. It comes when we have put off this mortal body and the evil tendencies that live in it. Paul calls it a "body of death" (Rom. 7:24). One day, praise God, we will shed these bodies and the presence of sin will be a thing of the past. Not only will Satan be forever banished from us, but even if he were not, there would be nothing in us to which he could appeal. In that day, everything about us will yearn for Christ alone. That is the future tense of salvation. We all share that blessed hope.

BUT FOR NOW

We're concerned for our **present** state. We live **today**. The presence of sin plagues us, therefore the present tense of salvation is before us. We feel the **power** of sin and don't like it. It is a battle and battles may be won or lost.

Observe. When I speak of Christian defeat, I do not mean the past tense of salvation. I mean the Christian's **present** failure to resist evil. To lose the battle to Satan means his domination of a life, not the forfeiture of heaven. This is an important distinction. Many "born-again" people are not being delivered from the POWER of sin. They are "born-again" because they **have already been** delivered from the GUILT of sin.

I know you are saved. You have given your heart to Christ. But Satan has lost more than one heart to Jesus, **yet managed to keep the mind.** This is why I mention the three tenses of salvation. Many a Christian has received a "new heart" at conversion, but kept his old head. People come to Jesus thinking, "It's all over now!" Moving down the aisle in response to the evangelist's call, they step out on the Lord's side. Their **fight WITH GOD is over.** Peace is declared. They feel it.

Yet, their **fight WITH THE DEVIL** is not over. Satan is not so concerned with those asleep in his arms, but when a man awakens in Christ, the war trumpet sounds. Some who thought "It's all over now," are shocked to find a **new conflict** before them. They heard, "Come to Jesus and everything will be all right!" Well, coming to Jesus is like enlisting in the army. God's people are both sons and SOLDIERS!

Once a man comes to Jesus, the power of evil moves as never before. The battle rages for control of his thought life. The new life requires a **disciplined** mind. God expects a complete shift in thinking, **"Let this mind be in you which was in Christ Jesus"** (Phil. 2:5). Satan moves to prevent that with a terrific onslaught of suggestion. The last thing in the world he wants is a changed mind which produces a changed life.

 "And be renewed in the spirit of your mind" (Eph. 4:23 KJV).

Do you know that verse? Satan hates to let go of a heart, but how pleased he is when he can hang on to a Christian's mind. His fight to dominate God's people by the **power of suggestion** is furious. Multitudes permit his domination long after they have come to Christ. They are ignorant of his working. Sadly, that dominion lasts until they take up the fight against him. *"Onward Christian Soldiers"* is more than a song — **it is a battle cry!** How many know they must "RECOVER THEMSELVES out of the snare of the devil?" (2 Tim. 2:26).

THE MILL OF THE MIND

 Along the shores of the North Sea you see the windmills. A perpetual breeze turns the massive fans. Inside, the huge wheels grind away. Feed grist into the mill and you get flour. If you don't, the great stones turn anyway. They are ready to grind whatever you supply.

The mind is a running mill. It never stops. Feed it with thoughts of Jesus and it grinds out His image. Feed it God's precious Word and the thought life produces a constantly changing man. The more a Christian's mind occupies with the things of the Lord, the more his life will change. On the other hand, feed the mind-mill with thoughts of this world and you produce a worldly man. Offer the mill a steady stream of THINGS and you get an unchanged man. Get a man to think of self only and he forgets Christ, **fast.**

The Christian who pays little attention to the mind-mill has an adversary eager to feed it for him. Satan is ready with endless **suggestions** for the thought life. This is how he exercises his dominion over us. Since he cannot touch our WILLS, he must work with something that **INFLUENCES** THE WILL. A man's thought life so affects his will he is said to be the product of his thinking. Remember the Holy Spirit's comment, "As a man thinketh, so is he!" Satan's power over the Christian remains as long as the devil is allowed to feed the mind-mill.

Satan's dominion does not always mean a life of gross sins. More often it is the opposite. The Satan-controlled Christian can live a very moral life, but **always a wasted one.** What he seeks is to make the life **useless to Christ** and he doesn't care whether it takes trash or treasure. Whatever accomplishes the destruction — **even religion** — is all right with him. That is his way of hurting God — making our lives **waste.**

THEREFORE the distinguishing feature of a Satan-ruled Christian is his UNCHANGING LIFE. He may go to church, observe the moralities, fit beautifully into society, and be a fabulous family man, but he **doesn't change!** Such a Christian is respectable, but hours pass with NO consciousness of the Lord's ambitions for him. It never occurs to Him that each day is to be squeezed for what it can produce in Christlikeness. His eyes are not looking for new ways to declare Jesus or exalt Him. Everything is seen as it relates only to himself. These Christians are "good people," even religious, but not changing **daily** into the likeness of the Lord.

DEAL WITH THE DEVIL

When Satan is allowed to feed suggestions into the Christian's thought life, spiritual growth is thwarted. Therefore, it is the plan of God for us to deal with the devil. Salvation DOES NOT include **automatic** victory over Satan. The glad news that ". . . greater is HE that is in you, than he that is in the world,"* makes victory **possible,** but there is **nothing automatic** about it, nothing which makes us immune to satanic attack. In fact, the New Testament teaches the opposite, that we are highly vulnerable.

---

*1 John 4:4

If we had any immunity our Lord would not have cautioned "WATCH AND PRAY." Neither would the Apostle Paul have bothered to list "the weapons of our warfare." Clearly we are in for a fight, a vicious fight for the usefulness of our lives. We are not guaranteed victory, we are guaranteed a **fight!**

Is it not Bible-mockery to read of our weapons and then fail to use them? Indeed. The Christian who fails to take up arms against Satan is already defeated. His lack of resistance invites satanic control. There can be no victory in the Christian life without a fight. We read:

"... and this is the victory that triumphs over the world, the faith that we have" (1 John 5:4 MLB).

At first reading it sounds like we have only to believe something and Satan is overpowered. Anyone who thinks that, fails to see that faith itself is a weapon. Paul called it a shield. A shield is a weapon and no good unless it is used. When it is used, it has to be raised **in time.** Even before you raise the shield of faith against "the fiery darts of the wicked," YOU HAVE TO SEE THEM COMING.

This is a military campaign. As such, it requires a definite plan. Unmethodical warfare is ridiculous. Without a well ordered plan for dealing with the devil, defeat is certain. Even though we are talking of the present tense of salvation, defeat is no light matter. People tend to relax knowing they are delivered from the GUILT of sin, but it is desperately urgent they also be delivered from the **power** of sin. That's what the judgment seat of Christ is all about. Our lives are going to be appraised on the basis of what we have done for

Christ. If we allow the enemy to make our lives empty, it will go hard with us in that day. The consequences of our Master's judgment will be ETERNAL.

I am saddened by the numbers who look upon Satan as a doctrinal trinket. Few have any thought for his ability to influence and control lives. As I said in the beginning it annoyed me that no systematic method for dealing with him has been given to God's people. Now I praise His name that He also has "annoyed" me to bring out this simple plan. May He use it to let even the newest Christian . . .

". . . withstand in the evil day, and having done all, to stand" (Eph. 6:13 KJV).

Chapter Three

THE WAR IN
THE MIND

"But I see a different law in the members of my body, waging war against the law of my mind, and making me a prisoner of the law of sin which is in my members."
(Rom. 7:23 NAS)

The Lord had His own precious way of teaching me about Satan. Some years ago, two inspectors from the city called at our chapel headquarters. They roamed over the property viewing all the facilities the Lord has provided. Then they shook their heads and smacked their lips.

"Tsk, tsk, we never dreamed anything like this was going on here. You are not zoned for this kind of an operation. Why, even the city doesn't have a printing plant like you people have. This whole thing will have to be reviewed. We'll let you know what we decide."

After all these years, two men come by from the city making statements which threaten the ministry. We had done all we could to secure approval from the planning commission, even to the point of public hearings, etc. But here was the threat just the same.

It didn't bother me much during the day. My hands and eyes are busy then. But at bed time, when things shut down, it was a different story. Hands are idle, eyes no longer scan. The mind has nothing to do but — THINK. That's what I did. At once my mind went to the two men from the city and began to meditate on the implications of their threat. What if this . . .? What if that . . .? All sorts of ifs and problems marched in review . . .

WORRY

If you don't think C. S. Lovett ever worries, you should have seen him that night. I tossed and turned and thought. The scene flashed through my mind again and again in endless succession. Every word that was spoken, all the hazards and possibilities. I concluded there wasn't anything I could do about it. Jesus would have to take care of it. I determined to let Him have it. He'd have to take the burden from me, if I were to get any sleep that night. My determination seemed strong yet the problem stayed on. I was serious enough to get out of bed and kneel down in a formal commitment, reminding the Lord that He had told me to "cast" my cares on Him. **And I meant it.**

Then I got back into bed — **and worried.** My mind was working like a typewriter. You know how wildly the keys fly to reach the end of a line. You shove the carriage back and start over. You do another line and shove the carriage again. My mind was working like that. I'd go through the problem, come to the conclusion I couldn't do anything about it, commit it to the Lord and start the process all over again. It was just like typing a line — bang — the carriage flies back for a fresh start.

The threat really wasn't that serious. There was no reason to lie awake fussing about it. I knew by faith that the Master had His own solution. But the worry process continued — for hours. It was getting more unreasonable by the minute. Then it hit me.

"Of course! Someone else has to be in on this! I'm being acted on by an outside force! This is way beyond anything I would normally do!"

That did it. Again the Holy Spirit moved within me. My mind returned to the situation that occurred at the foundation (see Introduction).

"Why didn't I see it sooner!"

Once more it was the difference between doctrine and practice. You see, I had already been alerted to the truth of Satan. Now I was meeting that doctrine in action. What an experience!

Most Christian psychologists agree that faith tends to make one a non-worrier. I will agree if that faith is directed both toward God **and Satan.** No longer can I feel that anyone will be a non-worrier by directing his faith toward God alone. I went through the experience of honestly committing my burden to the Lord and was prepared to forget it, when it began making return visits to my mind. It was not a question of my faith toward God. It was the problem of an intruder with power to keep my mind stirred up! An intruder as real as God! **My faith in Jesus did not get rid of Satan!**

ACTION

The **doctrine** of the devil didn't help a bit. I began to think about it, but that didn't rid me of his nagging. Then God's Word rose from deep inside my spirit like a surfacing submarine:

"Resist the devil and he will flee from you!"

I sensed His voice. The Holy Spirit was nudging me to act. Whew! Resisting the devil wasn't the same thing as resisting temptation. I had been resisting temptation for years, but resisting the devil as a living person, was new. You know how we all feel about facing something new and untried — shaky. And when I considered that he was "the god of this world," goose pimples appeared. I swallowed hard.

It was clear, I was going to have to take action. And it would have to be overt and definite. Satan's presence was becoming fearful. Sweat broke out on my hands. I thought I could feel his ugly breath. I began to tell the Savior I was afraid to do anything like that, perhaps He should do it. I even mentioned to the Lord the stories I heard of people asking Jesus to answer Satan's knock. But immediately His witness came to my heart:

"I've already dealt with Satan. Now it's your turn. But don't worry, he's a defeated enemy. He will flee if you resist him in My name!"

Of course, I didn't hear sounds of articulate speech, that message came from deep inside me. It was clear. The ball was in my hands. It was time to act. But what to do? My mind raced to the scene where our Lord Jesus was tested of the devil. **He talked to him.** He told him, **"Get thee hence!,"*** probably the equivalent of

---

*Matt. 4:10 KJV

our "Beat it!" Then He followed it with a quote from God's Word.

I didn't see how I could go wrong following the example of the Lord Jesus. Okay. I'd try it.

Margie was asleep. Had been for hours, so she didn't hear me. I let the words out.

"Satan! In the name of the Lord Jesus, GO AWAY! For it is written, 'Be anxious for nothing, but in everything by prayer and supplication with thanksgiving, let your requests be made known to God. And the peace of God which surpasses all comprehension, shall guard your hearts and your minds in Christ Jesus!' "*

Then I covered my head. I guess I thought the ceiling would fall in. I was ready for anything. It was so new to me. I thought Satan might even hit me. Nothing like that happened, so I thanked the Lord saying, "I did it, Lord Jesus, just like You said."

Know what followed? Within minutes I was fast asleep.

THE NEXT MORNING

I awoke refreshed, but terribly impressed. Something wonderful had happened. I had tasted the thrill of having Satan flee! What an experience! I was almost "high" with the idea of having power over Satan. Then I was humbled when I realized it wasn't my name he feared, but that of our precious **Lord Jesus!** Oh, that wonderful name! A new respect for the **authority of Jesus' name** swept over me.

---

*Phil. 4:6, 7 NAS

61

Victory in the thought war. That's what I had tasted. The enemy had been free to guide my thinking and use normal anxiety as emotional fuel. I was worrying when I didn't **want to,** worrying when I knew I didn't **need to.** I had committed everything fully to Christ. Some will think I didn't really make the committal, but not so. I did. What I had failed to do was **resist** the one who had the power to do such things, **regardless of any committal!** The presence of Jesus did not get rid of Satan!

What a simple word — **resist.** I didn't have to conquer, match wits or even be smart — just resist. And Satan fled! Victory through Christ took on a new look!

NEW ADVENTURE

The thrill of my experience was intoxicating. Victory in the Christian life loomed a tantalizing reality. True, I was like a baby learning to walk. This was a new action area for me. I wanted more. The pressure release was glorious. I have written a book featuring the two natures of the believer **(DYNAMIC TRUTHS FOR THE SPIRIT-FILLED LIFE),** but the truth of any pressure release from the carnal nature wasn't included. Now it had happened to me.

It was akin to my first soul-winning experience. I remembered the first time a person bowed his head and said "YES" to Jesus as the result of my work. It was enough. I was hooked. The thrill of it was like dope, I wanted more. Now a similar joy had occurred. This could only be the beginning of a bold new adventure in Christ.

REFLECTION

I sat on the edge of the bed awhile before getting up. I wanted to review that fantastic thing. Here was a moment in my life as big as salvation — almost. Victory in the Christian life is something to yearn for. Now it appeared I had received the key. The Lord was in it. The timing, the inner workings of my mind, the circumstances were just right for Him to teach me the mechanics of resisting Satan.

"Why didn't I realize this sooner!"

Working with the Holy Spirit wasn't new to me. If you have read, **SOUL-WINNING MADE EASY,** or **WITNESSING MADE EASY,** you know I teach the precise science of working with Him **at close range.** As I meditated and reviewed the experience, insight broke over me.

"That's it," I almost shouted.

This time Margie did hear me. She was already up and dressed.

"What did you say, Honey?"

I blushed a bit. How could she possibly know?

"It's nothing, dear."

Nothing! It was so big I didn't know how to tell her. Besides, I needed time to think it through. I'm not sure what she would have thought had I tried. I was too effervescent, too full of spiritual wonder to explain anything just then. Later I would.*

THE SATAN BUTTON

That loud exclamation was my response to spiritual insight. Suddenly I knew what had happened. It was precious. Even obvious, now that I thought about it.

● Do you remember the power-steering illustration on page 30 of **WITNESSING MADE EASY?** In spite of the presence of a power unit on the car, nothing happens until you turn the wheel. Well, a lot of things are power-operated today. I'm thinking of my garage door. I push a button and up it goes. I don't even press hard. An electric motor does all the work for me. But **until I push,** nothing happens.

Resisting Satan is like that. We have within us the Mighty One. He has met Satan head-on, suffered the worst he could deliver and defeated him. One Whose very name shakes up the spirit world. One Whom Satan

---

*Incidentally, the City Clerk called that morning asking me to forget about the visit. Some paper work had gotten mixed in the planning office. But now everything was straightened out. Accident? I should say not. The Holy Spirit obviously arranged the experience as a teaching device. He does things like that, doesn't He, just to teach us the stupidity of worry.

64

dreads and from Whose power he will flee! You see it is not the presence of the Lord in our lives that puts Satan to flight — **but His power!** And His power is not operative **until we resist.**

To resist Satan is like pushing the button for my garage door. One touch, one actual touch and power moves to do the job. One bit of resistance, one overt act of resistance and the power of God does the rest.

It is obvious, of course, that Satan does not flee from C. S. Lovett. Far from fearing me, he maneuvers me all over the place. He exploits my old nature and weaknesses continually. But if by deliberate choice I press the ANTI-SATAN BUTTON, the flashing power of my indwelling Savior operates to make him flee. If I don't press the button, there's nothing automatic about the presence of Jesus to hinder the tempter's working. If I don't resist the devil in person, nothing in this world can make him flee.

That's no slight bit of information.

SO WE'RE BUTTON PUSHERS

Take another look at the quote:

"Greater is He that is in you than he that is in the world."

It is not by accident that John says, "he that is in the world." The world is Satan's. He is the ruling giant. This verse is comparing the might of two giants. It is **NOT** teaching that Christians are **automatically** victorious, because the mightier One lives within them. NO . . . only that they **can be.**

See the whole verse in that light.

"Ye are of God, little children and have overcome them, because greater is He that is in you, than he that is in the world" (1 John 4:4).

Notice who does the overcoming. We do. Christians are the overcomers. The indwelling Christ is the **means.** Again, it is like my garage door. A 1/3-horsepower motor indwells my garage. That motor is greater than the door. It can make my door go up and down. But the **presence** of the motor doesn't automatically do this. It is the **power** of the motor. Until I press the button, there is no power. See it? Nothing happens until I press the button.

Yes, the Mighty One of heaven lives within us. He is our spiritual Motor, installed at Salvation, if I may reverently say so. He supplies all of our power for spiritual action. It doesn't matter whether it is **witnessing or resisting Satan,** it has to be done in the power of our Heavenly Motor. And this Motor doesn't operate **until we press the button.**

What is the button? Words. **Spoken words.** When we speak to the lost souls around us, the button is pressed. God's power goes with our witness. When we speak to Satan, God's power makes him flee. It doesn't matter whether we are **witnessing** or **resisting,** words from our mouths press the button. We act first, then God acts. "Go and Lo," applies to resisting the devil as well as witnessing to the world.

AUTOMATIC VICTORY?

If the presence of Jesus in our lives provided an automatic buffer against Satan, then it should also be an automatic soul-winning device. We know that isn't so. A man in the closest kind of fellowship with the Lord **does not** automatically win souls. He has to take action. He has to **speak** to lost men. He must make some overt move, he must present Christ in some way or there is no witness at all. A close relationship with Jesus does not get rid of Satan. Those who are the closest to Him often feel the most penetrating darts of the wicked one. Some find that the closer they get to Jesus, the more they are harrassed by Satan.

The point? The presence of one person in our lives doesn't get rid of another. Pre-occupation with Jesus does not get rid of Satan. Even though our Lord is mightier than the devil, His power is but the **means** by which we **can be** rid of our enemy. To occupy with Jesus and ignore Satan, simply gives him the freedom he needs to exploit the weaknesses of our flesh.

If that is so . . .

We truly have a **personal** adversary, one who lurks about looking for ways to stir up our old natures. He neither slumbers nor sleeps. No wonder the Master taught us to pray . . .

 "And lead us not into temptation, but deliver us from the evil one" (Matt. 6:13 ASV).

The danger is real. His presence is real. His powers are fantastic and not cancelled by the presence of Christ within us. The situation is serious enough for our Savior to ask:

 "I pray Father, that Thou wouldst keep them from the evil one" (John 17:15).

So I sat on the edge of the bed, my mind exploding with the impact of insight. The Spirit of God was teaching me about Satan. From that moment on, I would think differently about the devil. It was a turning point. Since then I have focused hard, experimented and counseled with the Lord, earnestly. You are enjoying the result.

How can Satan make us worry? How is he able to make us to go over a problem again and again, even when we know it is useless? That is before us now.

HOW SATAN ATTACKS THOUGHT LIFE

If Satan has access to our minds, by what means does he exercise control over them? Is he able to reach in and manipulate our thoughts to make them coincide with his own? Is he allowed to interfere with our choice of thoughts? Can he impose his thinking on us in violation of our free will?

Never!* God denies Himself that privilege. The entire human program is based on man's freedom of choice. The faith method would collapse without it. For faith is our free, human response to divine revelation. You can be sure Satan is not allowed to trespass limits God has placed on Himself.

But don't feel sorry for Satan. He doesn't want to control our thought life by **imposing** his own. If he did

---

*Demon possession does not occur involuntarily, except in cases of brain damage or disease. LSD may lead to it, but it is taken voluntarily. A small percentage reside in mental institutions due to a diseased condition of the brain. Most have what is called or rather miscalled a "nervous breakdown," with a long history of permissiveness prior to the personality collapse. Such conditions arrive gradually, with the victims consenting all the way until control is passed to the devil. Demon possession does not occur overnight and never in violation of the will. However, one can surrender his will to Satan seeking his control, just as he can surrender to the Holy Spirit permitting His control.

that, we would no longer be responsible for the foul and selfish imaginations we entertain. He wants us judged for the wickedness he inspires. Therefore, he wants us free to act on his suggestions. That way he·can turn around and become our accuser as well as the tempter.

So both want us to exercise the freedom of choice. Satan wants us to **choose** evil so that we will be judged for it, and God wants us to **choose** to do right so that we can be rewarded for it. Both want us to serve them **by choice.**

SATAN'S ADVANTAGES

If we review the tremendous advantages of the adversary, we can see **how** he is able to enjoy his remarkable power over our thought life. I'll list them briefly. It will help for you to think of his powers as similar to those of the Holy Spirit. Since he operates in the spirit, the "god of this world" sees as God sees:

1. **Instant and immediate access to each person's mind.**

2. **Complete panorama of our thoughts and imaginations, including motives, intentions, and secret ambitions and longings.**

3. **Familiarity with every weakness and strength, particularly our defenseless and vulnerable areas.**

4. **As permitted, either by carelessness or ignorance, he can plant or remove ideas from our minds.**

Should we respect an enemy who can do that? You bet. He knows us better than we know ourselves. We like to forget our mistakes and pass over our faults, but he doesn't. Every weakness and passion is tucked in his memory bank. That fantastic intelligence of his, gained

69

through thousands of years in the people-business, makes him at home in every nook and cranny of our fallen natures.

CONTROL BY SUGGESTION

That's how it is done, you see. **By the power of suggestion.** This is a skill. And in the hands of someone expert in human weakness, it is an **awesome** power. Let that someone be a genius in designing approaches to human vulnerability and he can master men. Man is a suggestive being. He responds to suggestion. God made him that way. God is in the suggestion business, too. Revelation is suggestion. Human response to divine revelation is **faith.** Human response to satanic suggestion is **sin.**

Make a suggestion to a man that matches his passions and appeals to his weaknesses, do it at the right moment and he is likely to buy it every time. Not that he HAS to, he WANTS to. That's where Satan's strength lies. His knowledge of human frailty gives him the ability to present the most appetizing suggestions. Proof that he is limited to the power of suggestion, is his use of wiles. Wiles would never be needed if he arranged people's thoughts arbitrarily.

Now most of God's suggestions have to do with the future. Many of them are unseen promises. All of them involve some denial or persecution of the flesh. It is easy to see why men would listen to Satan's ideas quicker than God's. The popular saying, "A bird in the hand is worth two in the bush," shows their thinking. It is a rare fellow who discounts the present for the sake of the future. Most want their cake right now. When you come right down to it, how many are interested in suggestions that squash the ego, deny the passions and overrule the instincts of the body?

So, don't feel sorry for Satan. He's got much going for him. He makes grand use of his long experience with

70

human weakness. With subtle genius and a treacherous heart, he lures people into evil by offering bait which appeals to their weaknesses. His skill lets him design evil suggestions so cleverly they not only match men's weakest points, but they often appear the righteous thing to do. His lies are so adroitly presented, they arrive in our minds as though they were the truth.

 If you are shocked that Satan has such enormous power, good. You should be. Remember, he made even our Master sweat drops of blood in the garden! Imagine what must have been the power of his suggestion that day! Whew! He knows we'll look long at any idea which fits our passions and ambitions. And if counterfeit, deception and disguise can make those ideas appear right for us, he knows we'll find our **own reasons** for going along with them.

THE VOICE OF SATAN

Did you ever hear the voice of God? I mean, have you ever heard Him state His will aloud? No. You have never heard His voice as **sound**. You don't hear Satan's voice either. Spirit-beings have no mouth. They don't need one. Eyes and ears are useless for spirit-to-spirit communication.

Still, we do hear them, because they have **another way** of presenting their suggestions to our minds. Only in recent times have we been able to understand how. Psychology, far from being the enemy of faith, has turned a floodlight on what was once secret and mysterious in the spirit-realm. Clinicians today work to bring healing to non-physical disorders, because they know man is more than a body — much more. And we draw on this advanced knowledge to explain the working within the spirit of man.

Here is scriptural fascination . . .

 "The Spirit Himself bears witness with our spirit that we are the sons of God!" (Rom. 8:16).

When you learn the spiritual mechanics of that verse you will also discover how Satan **speaks** his suggestions. The Holy Spirit and the unholy spirit address our minds in precisely the same way. All contact with spirit beings is by means of our **own** spirit.

SATAN'S WITNESS

Satan uses exactly the same method as the Holy Spirit. His spirit bears witness with our spirit. We don't see or hear the "god of this world," any more than we see or hear the God of heaven. Yet he can put his "amen" to anything in our unconscious. He too can activate and trigger material causing it to pop into awareness as an idea. For example, you drive by a nice big home. The thought strikes, "I ought to have a house like that." Christians seldom suspect the true source of such an idea. The devil loves to saddle God's people with things which can hinder and drain their capacities for Christ.

Just because an idea strikes the mind, you don't have to accept it. You are free to reject the notion, but since it comes from within, you never suspect an **OUTSIDER** has anything to do with it. It appears to be your own idea, hence you are not suspicious. Therefore you are inclined to entertain it. You let it linger in your imagination. Rejecting ideas that pop into the mind is a discipline. One which Christians do not develop until they learn about the enemy who sows them.

 Let a trim, shapely waitress serve your table. You look. No harm in that, it is natural to behold beauty. But a more subtle notion enters your mind. A sexual one perhaps. Or one of dissatisfaction with your wife. Before you know it, a fantasy is fired in your imagination. One which God wouldn't approve. It is well developed before you realize it. I'm talking in terms of split-seconds. Even so you are free to reject or indulge in the evil idea. Satan has no power to keep that image before you if you **don't want it.** But he knows your **weakness.** You do want it. Oh, this outsider is clever.

THE CONSCIOUS AND THE UNCONSCIOUS

Consider an iceberg. The mind is like that. Icebergs are deceiving. Only ten percent of their bulk is above water. The rest sprawls beneath the surface. Our mental history is distributed about like that. The portion above the surface, we call the conscious. The remainder is the unsconscious, sometimes called the subconscious. Sub, means under. I will use the terms unconscious and subconscious interchangeably. One of them might be more familiar to you.

 The conscious consists of things of which you are aware right now. As you sit reading, you are aware of the book in your hand, your chair, what day it is. You know about your family. Anything that can pass through your mind right now, we call the conscious. Another word is awareness. Conscious-awareness represents a wee fraction of our mental history.

The subconscious a foul swamp

Sigmund Freud, the acknowledged discoverer of the subconscious, called it a foul swamp. After years of probing, unlocking mental secrets, he likened man's mind to turning over a rock. Vermin scurry in all directions. He worked extensively with dreams, the TV of the unconscious. His writings testify to the indescribable filth and evil of man's depraved, fallen nature.

The **conscious** has self-imposed restraints. Every person learns to discipline himself to some extent. One cannot live with people and not do so. This provides a veneer, a social conscience, a standard of living, which makes it possible for people to get along with each other. But below the line, it is a different story. Even in the politest of old ladies, the **unconscious** is a monster of hideous evil.

Satan has everything he needs in the unconscious. Yea, more than enough. He is well aware of **everything** on deposit, has insight to every weakness, appetite and desire. He knows exactly what ideas to send into your thinking so as to keep your mind from spiritual things. It isn't necessary for him to fill your mind with filth to accomplish this purpose . . . just things of the flesh. Since it is true, "As a man thinketh in his heart, so is he . . .," Satan's cleverly planted ideas can make a man of God **act like the devil.**

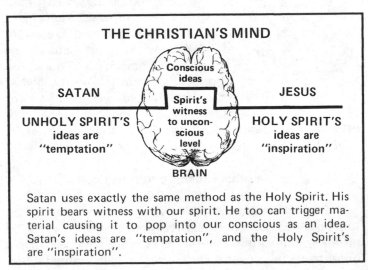

THE CHRISTIAN'S MIND

Conscious ideas

SATAN

Spirit's witness to unconscious level

JESUS

UNHOLY SPIRIT'S ideas are "temptation"

HOLY SPIRIT'S ideas are "inspiration"

BRAIN

Satan uses exactly the same method as the Holy Spirit. His spirit bears witness with our spirit. He too can trigger material causing it to pop into our conscious as an idea. Satan's ideas are "temptation", and the Holy Spirit's are "inspiration".

Behold the subtlety. Ideas arise within your own spirit. They coincide with your passions. That's what makes them so tempting. Ask yourself, **"Would I be inclined to resist a notion that meets a secret longing in my own soul?"** That's a valid question. Satanically spawned ideas appeal to the instincts. They purport to satisfy the longings of your soul, yet they cater **only to your fallen nature.**

DOES THAT MAKE FIENDS OF US?

When I say that Satan gets men to think as he does, I do not mean that they must become sex fiends or human exterminators. Ambition is equally useful for Satan's scheming. He uses **"godly"** ambition to satisfy the depraved wants of the Christian. Christian workers can be vicious, because viciousness is already on deposit. Of course, the suggestions never appear as being vicious. Godly men would reject them at once if they did. The happy prospect of accomplishing ambition makes good men blind to this evil.

Do gossiping Christians really mean to destroy others in Christ? Of course not. It doesn't occur to them that an evil need within them is being satisfied by a satanic scheme. The yearning to satisfy the need is so strong it blinds them to the hurt which follows. Who really suspects the words issuing from his mouth are often inspired by the unholy spirit? Gossiping is perhaps the most heinous, vicious crime of Christianity, yet multitudes do it and enjoy it. Ever hear a thoughtful Christian say, "I love to gossip?" Without realizing it, gossipers are used by the devil. Any such move to satisfy a depraved instinct, is always authored by Satan. Of all the unholiness in God's people, gossip is perhaps the most satanic.

75

Judgementalism is related to it. How quickly do you berate the person who doesn't agree with you? Do you repudiate the brother who follows the Arminian tradition because you believe in eternal security? You speak in tongues? Then what is that at the end of your nose? Oh, a brother who doesn't? It is easy to judge over doctrine. Satan can make a difference in doctrine appear as a personal insult. He knows how to twist even the tiniest difference into a declaration of war! He uses our most lofty feelings to clothe unholy suggestions. What an awesome enemy!

Having said that, you can see what an unforgiving spirit would offer Satan! The power he exercises over that Christian is enormous. The way he uses the tongue of the unforgiving Christian is unbelievable! Satan's own hatred for Jesus is put into words and used against other brethren whenever he finds the unforgiving spirit.

SUMMARY

1. The man who would have victory in the Christian life must do something about Satan. If he is allowed to operate unnoticed, his suggestions are powerful enough to control the life of any Christian. Victory through Christ is NOT AUTOMATIC. The indwelling presence of Jesus does not get rid of the presence of Satan. You protest, "Is not Satan a defeated enemy?" Indeed, but he is still an enemy.

He was defeated by the Lord Jesus. That defeat has nothing to do with us . . . UNTIL WE RESIST HIM. Unless we take overt action against the devil, he is not defeated as far as we are concerned. He is just the opposite, a mighty adversary who triumphs over us daily. It is when we move to resist him in Jesus' name, that he flees. Not until then.

2. Do Christians suspect that many of the ideas traveling through their heads are inspired by Satan? Very few. The power of Satan is unheralded today, almost unknown. Much we dismiss as "being human." Yet, a little reasoning shows that our minds have to be his prime target. "As a man thinketh in his heart, so is he!" is a truth which makes Satan desperate to control our minds. Obviously, the thought life is the real, spiritual battle ground.

3. Satan is the unholy spirit. The Holy Spirit is God. Both are in touch with us at the unconscious level. Either is able to use material on deposit in the subconscious and send it into our thought life AS AN IDEA. When Satan does it, it is called **TEMPTATION.** When God does it, it is called **INSPIRATION.** Since the ideas come from within us, we naturally view them AS OUR OWN. There is nothing on the surface to make us suspect that outsiders have produced them. Therefore, Christians need the discipline of examining their thought life and watching for Satan's influence.

This is why the Word of God says, "BRINGING EVERY THOUGHT INTO CAPTIVITY UNTO THE OBEDIENCE OF CHRIST." Far from being an impossible thing, it is, in fact, the only way to real victory in Christ! But such a thing can never happen until God's people become serious about their minds and Satan's power to control them with suggestions.

4. Satan is not allowed to violate our wills. He is limited to the use of suggestions. Unfortunately, the power of suggestion is one of the greatest forces motivating people. Satan is a master at it. His knowledge of human weakness allows him to design suggestions like no other. They not only correspond to our weaknesses, but promise to satisfy our longings, hence they are almost irresistible . . .

. . . UNTIL THEIR SOURCE IS RECOGNIZED.

That is the point of this book. Learning to recognize Satan's work in our lives and resist him. Wait until you see how cleverly he approaches us with his suggestions. Most would never suspect Satan has anything to do with the things which fill our minds all day, but he does. You'll see.

Chapter Four

SATAN'S SUPER DISGUISE

"Let us therefore lay aside the deeds of darkness and put on the armor of light." (Rom. 13:12 NAS)

Imagine a fire inspector — who is also a firebug!

He arrives at the scene in time to enjoy the blaze. See his warped satisfactions mount with the smoke and flames. When the investigation is conducted he knows where to look for the evidence **and erases it.** No one suspects his repeated presence at the fires, a fire inspector belongs there. With all clues removed, how long would it take to discover such a firebug? A long time? Indeed. His disguise is perfect. Who'd suspect a fire inspector — as a FIREBUG?

UNDERCOVER WORK

We have already noticed that Satan needs obscurity for his work. He depends on the cloak of **personal** dark-

79

ness. One of his greatest weapons has been his ability to convince people he doesn't exist. Because of this, he can do his work without any fear of being observed by God's people.

The Los Angeles Times recently carried a feature story by its religious editor, Dan L. Thrapp, who covered a conclave of notable Southland Theologians. The Rev. James Kallas, author of the recently published, *"The Satanward View,"* was credited with saying:

"I am fully convinced that Satan as an independent personality does not make sense in the 20th Century even though he is at the center of biblical thought" (L.A. Times, Sept. 4, 1966).

Don't you find this darkness startling when you consider that Satan speaks directly in the Bible three times! Once to Eve, once to God in heaven and then to the Lord Jesus. The New Testament writers had no doubt about him. Paul called him "the god of this world," the "prince of the power of the air," and "an angel of light." Peter referred to him as "a roaring lion." Jesus described him as the "prince of this world." John avowed that the whole world "lies in the evil one." Did not our Lord warn Peter that the devil was after him to "sift" him. As far as the Bible is concerned there is nothing vague or unreal about Satan.

 Why then do Christians treat him like Santa Claus? They smilingly employ cliches like, "the devil got in," yet wink at the real truth of his presence and power. How can Christians refuse to consider someone whose access to them is akin to that of the Holy Spirit? How can they ignore someone whose knowledge of human weakness and godlike power to exploit it allows Christians

"to be taken captive by him at his will?" Easy, dear reader. **He has a perfect disguise.** He is like the fire inspector who is also a firebug. No one would suspect Satan was behind this disguise.

SATAN'S PERFECT DISGUISE

So effective is Satan's disguise that he can acquire almost total dominion of a Christian's life, yet the victim doesn't suspect the identity of his evil master. The satanically led Christian doesn't give one thought to Satan. Yet, all the while the god of unrighteousness is ordering the steps of his life. You wouldn't think such a thing could happen to a Christian, but when you learn the nature of his disguise, you might blush. It could explain why your life in Christ isn't all you would like it to be.

His disguise?

Hang on for a surprise. The mask is . . .

 SELF

Reserve your chuckle until you see how it works. It isn't really funny. What could be more subtle than satanic suggestions which arrive in your mind as your own ideas?

Perhaps it has never occurred to you to look **beyond** your behavior pattern to see if someone has a hand in it besides yourself. There is someone. Just as our Lord Jesus turned to Peter and said, "Get thee behind me, Satan" — just as He stood in the boat and rebuked the one behind the storm — so must you learn to see the **unholy spirit** at work in your life. Behind most of our thoughts and actions is the evil one. Because of his disguise, we don't suspect his presence. It never occurs to us that someone else has the power to **engineer** our behavior without once violating our free will.

THE MASK OF SELF

Satan is a self-centered man. God said so. He got into trouble in the first place for saying, "I will be like the Most High." "I" trouble — the chief character of Satan is his preoccupation **with himself**. He lives for himself. He is completely selfish. Surely you have observed the "I WILLS" of his fall (Isa. 14:13-14).

> "I **WILL** ascend into heaven
> I **WILL** exalt my throne
> I **WILL** sit also upon the mount
> I **WILL** ascend above the heights
> I **WILL** be like the Most High!"

Enamored by his own beauty, wisdom and power, Satan was sold on himself. He actually, "thought it not robbery to be equal with God." Such thinking moved him to go after God's throne. But God cleared the air quickly:

 "Because thine heart is lifted up and thou hast said . . . I sit in the seat of God; yet thou art a man and not God, though thou hast set thine heart as God" (Ezek. 28:2).

That did it. The spirit in Satan was in direct conflict with the Spirit of God. Satan had to go. Jesus reported his banishment:

 "I saw Satan, as lightning, fall from heaven" (Luke 10:18).

There it was, the **spirit of Satan.** Full of self-will, self-exaltation, self-satisfaction. Wherever you find it, the **spirit of self** is the spirit of Satan!

WHEN MAN FELL

The ground was cursed the day Adam fell. But that wasn't the worst of it. Adam's nature was **shaped** that instant. Until that moment Adam was innocent. But now he had **knowingly** exalted his will against God, **just as Satan had done.** Adam joined the Satan rebellion that day. The same spirit that was found in Satan could now be seen in Adam. It could also be said of Adam:

 "Thou wast perfect in all thy ways from the day thou wast created, till iniquity wast found in thee" (Ezek. 28:15).

The same sin. The same result. Cast out.

The fall of man and the enterance of sin into the human race forces God to deal with men as sinners.

Thus all men since Adam are born under satanic control. All inherit the "spirit of disobedience" from their ancestor. "For by one man's disobedience, many became sinners" (Rom. 5:19). The Law of the Harvest stands. Sinners can only beget sinners. The creation was sold out. Satan became the master of all men.

Even in the fall, man's freedom of choice is protected. Satan has no control over man's will. His dominion is limited to suggestions. Yet, man's fallen nature guarantees his devilish mastery. He rules the sons of men by virtue of his **access** to their fallen natures and clever **appeals** to their passions. Now to see how this works and penetrate Satan's super disguise.

THE SAME SPIRIT

When Adam elected to disobey God, his spirit became like that in Satan . . . a **self-exalted spirit.** Thus the spirit of Satan is **identical** to that in fallen man. This is the KEY TO HIS DISGUISE. Every Christian has this fallen, sinful nature and is shot through with the spirit of disobedience. When he receives the Holy Spirit at salvation, a new nature is created in him, but that **doesn't get rid of the old one.** If it did, living for Christ would be a snap. Automatic, in fact. Of course, there'd be no growth either. Christians mature only as they live under the stress (struggle) of their two natures.

● I grind no doctrinal axe in this book. I want to avoid all the theological toes I can. Victory in Christ is bigger than any of our theological terms, so when I refer to the spirit in man as being sinful, fallen, adamic or satanic, those are simply my words to describe it. You may have another label more compatible with your theology. Good. Use it. But regardless of any names we use, I am talking about the surging spirit in all of us that is so eager to **assert itself.** You can recognize it as the inner desire to talk when someone else is talking; or tell of your experience when someone else is describing his; or of your impatience to explain something when another is telling how he does it.

We all have this spirit. Certain lip phrases give it away:

"I can't see how anybody would want to . . . . "
"You ought to see how I do . . . . "
"I don't care what anyone says, this it the way I. . . "
"You'd think he'd know better than to . . . . "
"Let me tell you what I'd do . . . . "
"If I were you, I'd sure . . . . "
"I always do it this way . . . . "
"You know what I think a person ought to do . . . . "

You could supply many more and each would be a gem of self-assertion. This is what I am calling the fallen, adamic nature, the "old man." You call it whatever you like. Put your own words in place of mine and theological fur will remain unruffled. We are identifying something by its **operation** instead of a theological name. It's more accurate anyway.

If the spirit in man is one of . . .

SELF-assertion, SELF-exaltation, SELF-satisfaction, SELF-glorification;

And the spirit in Satan is one of . . .

SELF-assertion, SELF-exaltation, SELF-satisfaction, SELF-glorification;

THEN . . . the two are identical. The spirit of man and the spirit of Satan coincide. And if they are identical, a man filled with the spirit of Satan does not have to be a Satan worshipper, but A SELF-WORSHIPPER! There! That's the big discovery.

85

THE FILLING OF THE SPIRIT

In my congregation is a young lad, a devotee of baseball. He is a little leaguer. When the world series ran he came to church dressed in his baseball outfit, a glove on one hand and a small transistor radio in the other. His pocket was stretched by a ball. He didn't hear my message. His ear was glued to that radio. He refused to miss one word of the announcer's description of the game.

 Now, that boy was **filled with the spirit of baseball**. He thought baseball. He talked baseball. He even took his bat to bed. It was all he cared about. You could say he ate and slept baseball. It possessed him. He was filled with it. It was his life.

As I am writing, civil rights is a big issue in our land. There are people filled with the spirit of equal liberty. They don't have time for anything else. They are consumed with a desire to march. Nothing else matters. They eat, sleep and dream civil rights. Their money, time, talents and energies are exhausted as they pour themselves into the struggle for equality. They are **filled with the spirit** of equal status for all men. Maybe some of you are involved. If so, you know what I mean.

The man filled with the **Spirit of God** is like that. He has a one-track mind. Ask him about politics and he'll answer, **"For me to live is Christ!"** He is reluctant to speak of anything else. **"This one thing I do . . .,"** summarizes his whole outlook. He means it. Nothing matters but living for Jesus. He eats, sleeps, and dreams Christ. The Christ-life is all he wants to talk about, think about or do. It affects his speech, the neatness of his dress, the way he conducts his business, pays his bills and carries out the routine of life. The man completely filled with God's Spirit is interested in things only as they relate to Jesus. His life is ordered by the single passion of exalting his Savior. It matters little what others think, he lives solely for his Master. From the moment he awakens until his eyes close in sleep, the glory of Christ is his occupation. Nothing can divert him, for nothing else matters.

Do you know anyone like that? I don't. But I would like to be that way. And so would you. Wouldn't it be glorious if your only longing was to shout the glory of Jesus! But alas, **another spirit** competes for our surrender. If he were not around, what publicity we could give to our Lord. But Satan lives! And his spirit moves **freely** in and out of our old nature. More often than we care to admit, we yield to the **leading of his unholy spirit.** Consequently most of us are far from what we long to be in Christ. Oh, to display the same passion for Jesus that my little leaguer showed for baseball!

NO ONE IMMUNE

A curious thought strikes your mind. **"Would a man filled with God's Spirit be immune to satanic attack?"** That is, would the same influence of the unholy spirit bear upon him? You can answer that. Consider our Lord Jesus. He was filled with the Spirit from the moment of birth, yet His life was under **continual attack** from the wicked one. The filling of the Holy Spirit did not eliminate **the presence** of the unholy spirit.

But there was something about Jesus which is not true of us. We cannot say:

 "The prince of this world cometh and hath nothing in Me" (John 14:30).

Far from it. We have sinned. We have disobeyed by choice. We have lived for ourselves. We have exalted ourselves and gratified our souls with the things of this world. Consequently Satan has EVERYTHING in us to which he can lay hold. Our old nature is still a part of Satan's gang. Our old man is still a disobeyer living in the lusts of the flesh, fulfilling the desires of the flesh (Eph. 2:3).

We are full of things Satan can touch and trigger. But someone protests, **"Hey, our old man is crucified with Christ and the former things are passed away!"** My friend, every dirty joke you have heard or told is on file in your unconscious. Every filthy thought you have ever tolerated is there too. Every bit of **envy, lust** or **jealousy** you have entertained is stored also. Watch, even in the midst of prayer some wicked thought or incident from your past will **flash into consciousness.** You'd better get a new interpretation for that verse. Some of the most dedicated Christians tell me it is a steady occurrence. Even in their most sacred moments, the trashiest of memories come to mind. There is **not a speck** of our wickedness that has passed away. Every bit of it is at hand for Satan to use. If you don't think so, watch the enemy at work.

Nothing is ever lost from our lives. Every evil thing we have ever thought, felt or been exposed to is recorded in the unconscious. Satan has access to it and uses it. But it was not so with our Lord Jesus. His personal purity, abhorrence of evil, refusal to disobey, left Satan nothing to use. Jesus never belonged to the disobeyers, Satan has no claim on Him. Jesus was never snatched from Satan's kingdom. We were!

You say, was He not tempted? Indeed. And **"in all points like as we."** Yet He never once sinned. That is the difference between Him and us. Nothing was lacking in His temptation. Even a man who has never once sinned can be tempted. Adam was like that. The very fact that our Lord was in a human body, made Him open to all the tests of the flesh. The fact that He is a Person, made Him susceptible to all the tests of pride. He suffered:

Physical hunger — **"Command these stones be made unto bread."**
Fear of death — **"Cried unto Him that could save Him from death!"**
Pride — **"The Kingdoms of the world in a moment of time."**

No, nothing was lacking in His temptation. Yet, there was nothing in Him that Satan could point to and say, **"This is mine!"** There is in us, **plenty!** We are sinners and Satan is king of sinners.

THE SATAN SPIRIT

A man filled with the spirit of Satan exalts HIM-SELF. The spirit of Satan **is** the spirit of SELF. Thus we can say . . .

The degree to which a man lives for himself is the degree to which he is filled with the spirit of Satan!

Conversely, the degree to which a man lives for Christ, that is the degree to which he is filled with the Spirit of God. That's a surprise? You expected the man filled with the spirit of Satan to go about talking of the devil? Don't blame you. The man who is filled with the Spirit of Christ goes about exalting Jesus. One would just naturally expect a Satan-filled man to exalt the devil to the same degree. **But it doesn't work that way.**

If the Satan-filled man went about declaring the devil, it would **ruin everything.** All of Satan's hopes would be frustrated. He can't afford to enter into open competition with the Most High. He doesn't dare risk open acknowledgment to receive worship as king of the rebels. The last thing in the world he would permit is a tent meeting where he is offered to men as the god of this world.

89

But doesn't he want to be worshipped openly? You bet he does. He longs for it. Aches for it. Anyone with his pride yearns to be openly declared as king. But there is something he wants more. What could it be? **To hurt Jesus.** That's right. Satan would rather hurt Christ than anything else. This is where his passion is directed. The cross of Christ, you see, destroyed Satan's future. His plans were shattered when the Prince of Glory died. Now Satan has nothing to look forward to but blackness. **Vengeance is what he wants now.** It's all that is left to him.

In my opinion, Satan would rather ruin **one Christian life** than rule a million unsaved souls. Lost people he has by the billions, but what is that? His kingdom ends. Blows against Jesus mean more now. Jesus is the target of his hatred, the object of his fury. In the years remaining to him, he is devoting himself to striking back at the One Who ruined his kingly ambitions. Public acclamation doesn't mean half as much as hurting Jesus. Since the Lord is beyond his reach, he must hurt Him **through His children.**

Thus Satan lives as the special enemy of the Christian.

OUR DEDICATED ENEMY

Satan's rage against Jesus makes him a dedicated enemy. He is relentless in his determination to destroy every Christian life. He knows how much the Master loves His own. Those of us with children know how we feel every pain that strikes our little ones. The Lord is like that. And Satan is keenly aware that any pain delivered against a man's child, hurts that man. The greatest hurt that can come to a child of God is living for SELF, instead of Jesus. When our Lord has to behold one of His own children living for the devil, it pierces His heart with the deepest anguish.

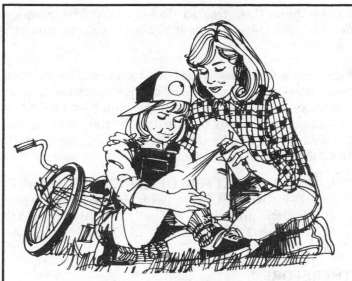

Those of us with children know that we feel every pain which strikes our little ones. Satan is keenly aware that the Lord feels every pain he can deliver to one of God's children. It's his greatest way to hurt our Lord.

The Apostle understood this:

"In my flesh I do my share on behalf of His body (the church) in filling up what is lacking in Christ's afflictions" (Col. 1:24).

Yes, Jesus still suffers. The battle between Him and Satan continues. Satan lives and the enmity persists . . .

"And I will put enmity between thee and the woman and between thy seed and her Seed; it shall bruise thy head and thou shalt bruise His heel" (Gen. 3:15).

The "heel" of Jesus is **still** being bruised, but Satan's headship was smashed. The devil's future was ruined, but he, himself, **is free** to do his worst. The cross was not his worst. **Hurt to us** is the most painful thing the Lord endures.

• So you and I, dear reader, are his target. To get to us, he must remain obscure. He cannot come to us as the enemy of the Lord, we'd have nothing to do with him. Put Christ and Satan before the Christian and ask him to choose. He'll take Jesus every time. Now for the real subtlety . . .

MAKE IT A MATTER OF CHOOSING BETWEEN CHRIST AND SELF . . . **(with all the deceptive power of Satan prompting the self)** . . . AND THE UNSUSPECTING CHRISTIAN CHOOSES SELF ALMOST EVERY TIME.

THEREFORE . . .

The devil willingly **forgoes public worship** if it will let him ruin God's people. He lives to cancel the Christian. He knows each born-again child of God has **just one life** in which to grow and develop into the likeness of Jesus. He also knows the Christian's future job in heaven depends on his faithfulness here on earth. So the enemy moves day and night to block the Christian's growth and render him useless.

Even in the day when Satan finally appears before mankind in person, it will **not be as himself.** He will sit in the temple of God **posing** as the true God and not in his own name (2 Thess. 2:4). He is a counterfeiter. To offer himself as the prince of demons and king of disobeyers would be foolish. No Christian would have anything to do with him. And since it is the Christian he seeks to control, he must hide behind the spirit of SELF.

SELF is the great mask of the devil. Satan lives. He is mighty. He is present. But hard to detect behind this ingenious mask — SELF.

Isn't that clever? Yet, should we expect **a god** to act with less genius? And the more so when we recall our Lord Jesus made him and filled him with wisdom? No, we should expect him to be remarkable. But there is wisdom for us in this. The very fact that he is free, is proof that God is using him to accomplish HIS own purposes. He is our enemy only because **God permits it** and for our profit. If there were no use for the devil, you can be sure he would have left the scene ages ago. Our God is using him and with a wisdom that surpasses that of Satan. Who would dream of such a scheme for bringing sons to maturity? Only God.

● But now see the mask of **self** in operation. Get ready to blush a little.

SATAN'S MAN

Can you picture a Christian filled with the spirit of Satan! Ugh!, how awful! What Christian believes he could be remotely involved with such a thing? Very few. But there is the strength of Satan, no one suspects such a thing could happen. This very thing accounts for his fabulous success in controlling Christian lives. You'll see why when we look at the Satan-dominated Christian. You might even recognize him.

 He rises in the morning ready for a cup of coffee. The smells of breakfast are more tantalizing than a breath of prayer. They are even more inspiring since his stomach is clamoring for attention. He sees no reason to ignore that call. He eats what HE wants. Is there any reason why Jesus should be a part of that?

He wears what HE wants that day. Clothes are hardly a Christian matter. Then he stands before the mirror studying HIS face. Some muscles to admire too. Not bad. He feels HIS smooth skin. There's satisfaction there, but not through thanking God for that face. He's ready for the day. He says goodbye to HIS wife. Prayer together? No time. He's got to get to HIS car and go to HIS job. Where do you put Christ in a routine like that, except perhaps for a word of thanksgiving at the breakfast table. Satan allows that.

 So he's off to serve HIS employer. After all, that's where the money comes from for HIS family. That employer is important. HE must be pleased. The day goes by. A few conversations with the Lord? Indeed not, he's got to keep HIS mind on HIS work. That's what he's paid for. Well, how about a trip to the restroom to leave a tract? Hardly. What would people think should they find out? Well then, a few minutes for devotion at lunch time? No. He needs some recreation with HIS friends. I see, then no witness on the job at all. Witnessing may be all right for other Christians, but there's no way to work it on his particular job. He's definite about that. Sure, Jesus gets a passing thought now and then. Christians do have to think about Him once in a while. That's okay with Satan.

He goes back to HIS home. Eats what HE wants for dinner. Sits in HIS chair. Reads what HE wants. Turns on the TV to select what HE wants. Relaxes for HIS comfort. Goes to bed when HIS body is ready. Time for prayer. Too tired, got to get up in the morning ready to go.

● How does that routine sound to you? Fairly normal? Not too bad if that's the extent of his self-living. Oh, but he does other things. Watch.

He goes to the market. For Jesus? No, no, to buy what HE wants. You mean he went out of the house not once thinking, **"How can I make this trip count for Christ?"** I'm afraid so. You see the Satan-filled Christian goes to the store merely to get THINGS. That's all. He selects cans from the shelf as they appeal to HIS flesh. There's some small talk at the cash register (nothing about Jesus), then back to HIS home. What does going to the store have to do with Jesus? Do you think it enters his head that **Christ's ownership of his life** includes everything? He's not allowed to think such things. Satan doesn't want blood-bought men connecting a trip to the store with Christ.

Let's follow Satan's man other places.

He goes to the barber shop. To get a hair cut, that's all. Does he bring up Christ to the other fellow waiting or does he bury his head in a magazine? You know. He does exactly what Satan suggests. Then perhaps he leaves a tract concealed in the magazine so that someone else may discover it? Of course not. The Satan-filled Christian reads only for pleasure, he's "killing time." He's waiting his turn in the chair. The fact that he will one day answer for that time doesn't occur to him. Satan blanks out such thoughts, too.

 Then our Satan-filled Christian goes to the drug store. To witness for Christ? No sir, he needed something. His wife asked him to stop. That was his only reason. What's that got to do with Jesus? So he wheels into the gas station. Ah, this time to witness for the Lord? No, he's low on gas. You mean he isn't even thinking of Jesus? No, just HIS car. He goes out of his way to baby that car. Would he go out of HIS way to baby Jesus a bit? Sure, that's what Sundays are for. But during

the week HIS car is more important. He could go into the restroom and leave a tract. **"Forget it,"** says Satan, **"You've got things to do."**

One of them is going by the post office. Good, that's a swell place to leave a tract. Is Satan's man thinking of Jesus as he walks in the door? No, just HIS mail. He wants to see what might be waiting for HIM. And it's the same when he goes to the bank. The trip is simply to put in or take out HIS money. Ah, I see he has time to take a magazine from the news stand. Maybe he'll put a tract in there? Too bad, it didn't occur to him. He reads what HE wants. And it never occurred to him that Jesus had to look at those pictures too.

What of his trip to the department store, auto supply shop, stationers? There again he buys what HE wants. It's HIS money, he spends it as HE pleases. He does the same at vacation time. He goes where HE wants. In fact, vacations let him break away from CHRIST for a time. There HE can enjoy HIMSELF and forget about Jesus. After all, everyone should get away once in a while. Vacation for Christ! Are you kidding? Satan says, "Vacation from Christ." That's a time to put Church and Sunday school completely behind you while you enjoy life.

I see the Satan-filled man has a hobby. Even in the garage he does what HE wants. He needs something just for HIMSELF. Wow! That's funny, isn't it? Who else has he been living for? Certainly not Jesus.

I don't suppose you recognize this Christian. Likely you wouldn't even know any born-again person who would devote the routine of life to SELF like that. Probably you've never met Christians who go to the store just to buy **things** and who squander days, weeks and years in self-living. But I assure you they exist. You rub shoulders with them. For you see, these Satan-filled Christians also go to church.

That's what is so tricky. It fools them. They think they're dedicated to Christ because they never miss a Sunday and drop the 10% in the plate. If one makes it to prayer meeting regularly, he's sure he's part of the inner circle. And if he teaches Sunday school on top of that, well . . . what else is there? Should he be a pastor, you know that's as high as one can go in commitment to Christ, isn't it? The Satan-controlled Christian must be involved in the church, for that is how he measures his devotion to Jesus.

SATAN'S WOMAN

Now Christian women are different . . . aren't they? Let's spy on the Satan-filled housewife and see.

 There she is now, cleaning HER house. Is she talking to Jesus as she dusts? Is that a prayer list I see over her sink? Is she remembering others while her hands are busy with the dishes? Hardly. "Ding, dong," she runs to the door. "I wonder whom the Lord is sending my way?" Is that what she asks herself? Satan has another question, "I wonder who that could be?" Jesus isn't in her thoughts at all.

Follow her to the mailbox. Is her mind so filled with Christ she is looking for His hand in every letter? Oops, "Bills, bills, bills. Seems like we'll never get ahead!" But she does want to look nice. So she goes to the beauty parlor. To look nice for Jesus? Well, if you have to put it that way. Actually though, it is for HERSELF. Then other women.

How about her children? They have to go to school. She sees to that. They need an education so they can

97

"get ahead in the world" In the world? How about their getting ahead in Christ? What does she do about that? "Oh, I send them to Sunday school." That's nice.

Maybe Jesus will be glorified in her garden. It's His, isn't it? After all, He gives life to the flowers. No, that's her private satisfaction. It's HER garden. She has to have something that's her own, too. Perhaps the house is maintained so as to bring glory to Jesus? No, it's to keep up with the neighbors. "We can't have them thinking we're trash." As she washes the windows, no doubt she is rejoicing. "I love to wash windows because it reminds me that Jesus has made my heart clean!" Satan forbids that. Instead, he whispers, "Three more and then you'll be done. Whew!"

● Brother Lovett, are you trying to tell me that these fine Christian people live for themselves, because of Satan's influence? Exactly. Remember the mask — SELF. You tell me who they live for. They eat what they want, go where they want, see what they want, do what they want, say what they want, spend their money any way they like, use their time as they please and squander their talents for peanuts. You can't tell me these fine Christians have seriously faced the call of God on their lives and know they owe all they are and have to Jesus?

How many trips will that man make to the gas station, the rest of his life? Thousands. Where does Christ fit in all that? Think of the conversations he will have in the years remaining to him. Shouldn't some words for Jesus come out? Think of the restaurants he'll visit, the trips to the bank, post office and stores! Can he leave Christ out of all that? What of the time spent going and coming from work, fixing his house, car and yard! Watching TV, reading the paper, visiting friends and enjoying outings. Wow! If Christ has no place in his daily routine, what's left?

 A few hours of church. After all, says Satan, isn't that what Christianity really amounts to — a gathering of Christians to sing and listen to the Bible? And so the Christian whose life is not his own, **is deceived** into thinking he's a dedicated man. The whole of his life down the drain, with enough religious interludes to make him think he's getting along in Christ. That's sad. What a testimony to Satan's power!

THE DISGUISE WORKS

All Satan has to do is deceive the Christian into **living for himself** and he frustrates God's ambitions. Satan's name is not mentioned. There's no hint of serving Satan in all this. Just self. This is what hurts God. He is painfully wounded when one of his children is led off like this. If the devil can keep Christians out of the Book, from prayer, from taking note of their own growth in Christlikeness, faithfulness in investing their time and money, he accomplishes his purpose. He rubs his hands with glee. When a Christian lives for himself, Satan jumps with ecstatic joy. He has hit God where it hurts most. For Satan, that is living. For the Christian, **it is living for Satan.**

It is easy for him to do this as long as he can work under the **disguise of SELF.** What Christian is about to **equate self with Satan?** That's like calling a fire inspector a firebug! Oh, does it work. He can plant all sorts of things in the Christian's mind and they appear as one's own ideas. He can get Christians to covet, boast, gossip, judge and condemn others; lust, waste their time, and all the while feel it is their own doing.

Never once do they suspect anyone is behind the mask of SELF. They just wish they were better Christians. Sadly they admit they fall far short of what they ought to be. Most know about the Holy Spirit and Christ's indwelling. They can't explain why they don't live for Jesus more than they do. How easily God's people are defeated. No wonder the Bible is full of warnings and cautions. No wonder the Apostle spoke so much about the **warfare of the Christian life.**

Satan's task is simple. He doesn't have to sell us on disobedience. He couldn't if the proposition were laid clearly before us. But he doesn't have to, He simply intensifies our SELF desires and we go out of our way to satisfy them. Getting us to live for ourselves, **is the same** as getting us to live for him.

SNEAKY SUGGESTIONS

When an idea arrives in your mind, what is there to make you suspect it is anyone's but your own? Until one knows about Satan's access to our minds and his method for planting suggestions, who suspects anyone but himself? Can anyone really believe an outsider is responsible for the thoughts in his head? Not until he takes God's Word seriously.

Satan can make you tired

You plan to go visiting for the church. You've already signed up. But the thought strikes, **"I'm too tired tonight. I think I'd better stay home. I'll go next week."** That sounds like your own judgment. But it isn't. The one who lives to render your life useless sent that notion to your mind. You're in a conversation. Some things coming from your lips are self-centered. Count the "I's." "I think, I always, if I were you, if you ask me, take me for example, etc." Watch yourself as others are speaking. How do you focus? Really listening, or thinking about yourself and what you're going to say next? Let a name come up. Is it someone with whom you dis-

100

agree or who has hurt you? Watch the feelings rise. What words are perched on your lips? How do you react when people disagree with you?

Did you know Satan can make you hungry?

You get up from the couch and head for the refrigerator. You stand before it knowing you don't need another thing in your stomach. Yet you open the door to indulge yourself. Why? Because you're hungry? Heavens no. The god of obesity makes suggestions which sound good to you. He's pleased to have your obedience in any area of life. Food is one of his favorites.*

He can make you lazy, too

Satan can make you lazy by suggestion. He can cause you to be dissatisfied with your wife, your house, your car, your job and your church. He can keep you on the go. He can get you to brag, boast and belittle others. He can do almost anything he wants with you. If you don't think so, start listening to yourself. And he exercises this dominion without touching your will. You will do all of these things because you want to. He sells you on a wile. He plants the suggestions. He times the temptation. And you act. Power? And how.

SATAN'S OTHER DISGUISES

His favorite and best disguise is self. He has two others which are whoppers. While this chapter is intended to bring out the truth of self, we shouldn't leave the matter of disguise without mentioning two more . . . PEOPLE AND CIRCUMSTANCES.

❶ People

Satan uses others to get to you. It is easy to see him use Peter in an attack on the Lord. Jesus had been tell-

---

* To overcome Satan's food stronghold in your life, see the author's book, "Help Lord — The Devil Wants Me Fat!"

ing the disciples how He must go to Jerusalem and be crucified, to rise again the third day. Peter spoke up, "Lord, let this thing be far from Thee!" Jesus, recognizing the real author of the suggestion, turned to Peter saying, **"Get thee behind me Satan!"**

Satan will use your dearest ones to hinder your life in Christ. An extravagant wife can pester a man to live beyond his means, driving him to the place where he has to **worry** about bills. That dilutes spirituality fast. Children can get into trouble to the point of causing anxiety and embarrassment. Well meaning friends can draw you away from a commitment already made to Jesus. The man of God has to watch for Satan in those closest to him.

 Even in death, Satan can use a loved one. At funeral time, Christians often behave as heathen. They spend huge amounts of money for caskets and flowers to honor a dead body, while the grand truth of being with Jesus is trampled in the dust. God's people often carry out a pagan farewell that makes it appear death really is good-bye. They splurge. Money which has been withheld from missions and Christian literature goes into the ground or supports a mausoleum. Watch Christians at funeral time. Do they really act as if physical death was a glorious transition into Jesus' presence or as if it were the end of everything? What a terrible testimony is presented when God calls a loved one. Yes, Satan uses **bereavement** to make fools of God's people.

❷ Circumstances

Satan has the power to arrange events in his world. He is the author of accidents, floods, famine and disaster. And God uses them all. In fact, our Father weaves the activities of Satan into His master plan so that every-thing works out for good. However, the devil is the sponsor of every destruction in this world. He cannot create, he can only destroy. He can arrange for that Christian, whom wealth would destroy, to make it. He can cause the Christian for whom money would be used to exalt Christ, to stay poor. He can engineer loss for one man and profit for another.

THE GREATEST WASTE

The deceived Christian, lured into **self-living**, produc-es the greatest waste of all. Behold the image of God, designed for the glory of God, feeding like bacteria in a dead body. So busy tearing at the carcass of this world, that he ignores the high call of living for Christ. Oblivi-ous to the great plan God has for him, such a Christian lets days, weeks and years go by, never dreaming his life is going down the drain. The day approaches when he will look back on this forfeiture with anguish.

"**Why didn't someone tell me?**" That won't work. I tell you now, Mr. Christian, to live for Christ. **Get seri-ous about Satan.** Learn to deal with him and brush aside his evil suggestions. Set yourself to serve Jesus and enter heaven a triumphant soldier. The greatest thing in this life is making the most of each day in preparation for the life to come. Why should you miss the best of your own faith? Even more provoking, why should you . . .

"Be ashamed at His appearing!"

You don't have to be. And you won't, if the next chap-ter starts in you what it is supposed to.

Chapter Five

GETTING READY
TO RESIST

---

*"Watch and pray so that you will not fall into
temptation. The spirit is willing, but the body is weak."*
(Matt. 26:41 NIV)

All animals have enemies. From mice to monkeys
WAR is the watchword.

Some African gazelles stop at a wilderness pool. See
how they listen — then drink. They look around first,
then drink. One in particular appears to be a sentry.
Then comes a sound — a twig SNAPS! The presence of
the enemy is known. The herd moves like a shot. It
flees with the wind. Seconds later could have been fa-
tal. Lives are saved because they — WATCH!

CHRISTIANS MORE VULNERABLE

Christians must watch for Satan. He is quicker than
a lioness hungry for gazelle. He travels with the **speed**

of thought. That is faster than lightning. As long as God's children are in the world, they must be on guard. Satan's world is enemy territory, a hostile place. Thus, Christians must look, then eat. Be on guard, then work. Listen, then play. WATCH, then pray. Watching, watching, watching — for they have less time than the stalked gazelle to escape their attacker.

The Christian's enemy is deadlier. What's worse there is no **natural** defense against him. Some animals enjoy protective coloration, others have quills and the skunk is unusually left alone. We are helpless in terms of any natural defense. Our enemy uses the natural means against us.

He triggers our natures and uses them. His suggestions appeal to our instincts. His ideas appear as our own thoughts. We can be captured by him and **not know it.** We can be used by him and **not suspect it.** We can be led to serve his evil ends and think we're godly when we do. He gets away with it, because it **is so natural.**

It's natural to want to get ahead in this world
It's natural to stick up for your rights
It's natural to take advantage of opportunities
It's natural to protect yourself
It's natural to want the best
It's natural to put yourself first
It's natural to clutch what's yours
It's natural to want a good time
It's natural to cater to appetites and passions
It's natural to place self and family ahead of others
etc . . .

SATAN USES EVERY NATURAL DESIRE TO ENSLAVE

When you harness the natural forces within a man, you have everything going for you. The new car salesman senses a prospect is drooling when he stops by his showroom. He need but picture that man in the car enjoying the prestige and pleasure of it and he'll start selling himself. Maybe you don't care about new cars. Then how about a new house, new dress, new job, new woman? I'm sure you have drooled over something and know what I mean about selling ourselves.

Satan is more than a salesman, he's a magician — yea, even ventriloquist. This magician's ideas appear as our own. Who turns down his own ideas? And when they appeal to one's dreams, ambitions and desires — Huummh? How ingenious to use what is **natural** in man to enslave him. No wonder he gets away with it.

SELF, SELF, SELF

You see it is self-ambition that makes a man plunder; like scheming for another man's job. It is **self-interest** that makes him exploit someone else; a girl perhaps. It is **self-satisfaction** that makes him gossip, blind to the hurt it produces. It is **self-pleasing** that makes him occupy with the things of this world. Satan knows how to get us all to live for ourselves by triggering the NATURAL desires. Can't you see how easy it is to lead Christians to **"do what comes naturally,"** when everyone else does it too?

NO WARNING

Have you heard of the DEW line? The United States has a string of radar sites stretched across the Arctic to detect approaching missiles and provide a warning for our military forces. Supposedly we have 10 minutes advance notice which would allow our government to launch an anti-missile offensive.

106

No Christian gets 10 minutes warning prior to satanic attack. He doesn't get 10 seconds. When Satan plants a suggestion in the thought-life, there isn't even a 1/10th second warning. There is NO WARNING. You have to be WATCHING for him all the time. To avoid the satanic snare, the Christian must:

1. Believe what God has said about this enemy.
2. Learn how his enemy operates.
3. Know of his enemy's weaknesses and strengths.
4. Have a definite plan for resisting his enemy.
5. Know how to use his own resources in Christ.
6. Go into action at the first hint of satanic suggestion.

This is a new way of life for the average Christian. It takes a bit of doing to get familiar with the anti-Satan defense system. Satan has enjoyed obscurity for so long, it requires **experimentation** before the average Christian discovers him ALIVE. It is one thing to read about him in this book, quite another to **meet him** head-on in your life. It's something like running across a rattlesnake lying coiled in your path.

Once you begin to resist the devil, your contacts with him are like collisions. You feel the bump. Then the warfare becomes more than a doctrine. Consequently this chapter has to do with the fight. It is not devotional, but a manual for war. When it does what it is supposed to, you'll treasure the name of Jesus as never before. Taste once what it is like to have Satan flee and the power of Jesus' name becomes **glory!**

WATCH AND PRAY

That is the Lord's priority in the matter:

 "Watch and pray that ye enter not into temptation; for the spirit indeed is willing, but the flesh is weak" (Matt. 26:41).

Here is PRE-TEMPTATION instruction. Watching comes **before** prayer. Once you fall into one of Satan's traps, it's too late for watching. Thus watchfulness is a part of our anti-Satan defense system, but it has no value AFTER one has succumbed to a satanic proposition. What good is the DEW line after missiles have reached New York or Los Angeles?

Before me is the account of a young minister who committed double murder on a Saturday morning and the following day entered his pulpit to preach from the text: **"Let the words of my mouth and the meditations of my heart be acceptable in Thy sight, O Lord, my strength and my redeemer."** What must have been the meditations of this young man's heart on Saturday? What words were in his mouth as the weapon fell on his victim? Can the most godly be duped by Satan through failure to WATCH?

Indeed, consider this young preacher. From what I can learn, he was soundly evangelical. Do you think his spirit was willing to do God's will? I do. Do you suppose he prayed as he saw the direction in which he was moving? You can be sure he prayed plenty. But did he WATCH? Watch what? Most likely he didn't know what to watch! Few do. And should he recognize the enemy, it's even more certain he wouldn't know what to do about it. Prayer wasn't the answer, he'd done that. His willing spirit wasn't the answer, he'd offered that to God. Obviously it was a case where a godly servant was ruined by Satan through the **weakness** of the flesh and **ignorance** of the devil.

RESISTING -- OUR JOB

In an earlier chapter I confessed that I once viewed, "Greater is He that is in you than he that is in the world," an **automatic** defense or armor against Satan. It seemed all I needed to do was stay close to Jesus and Satan couldn't touch me. I have since found it to be just the opposite. The closer I am to Jesus, the more fiercely rages satanic attack. After the most glorious victory in the Lord, there frequently comes a severe testing.

But if Jesus' presence is not automatic armor, **what is it?** It is a RESOURCE. If you will permit me, it is something we can use in our resistance of the devil. The name of Jesus is our **strength.** But like any strength, what good is it **unless it is used?** The verse, "Greater is He that is in you," is our ENCOURAGEMENT TO FIGHT. We are being told, **"Don't be afraid to stand up to Satan."** Why? Jesus says, **"I'm right here with you."** That should be like saying "Sic 'em" to your dog. But again you can see that even such a resource would be useless unless you SAW the enemy. So, **"WATCH and pray,"** is the urgent caution, "Greater is He that is in you," blessed assurance in the battle.

Now it is our battle. James says for US to resist the devil and he will flee from US. Nobody can do this for us. It is the same as **"Lay up FOR YOURSELVES treasure in heaven."** No one does that for us either. Clearly it is our fight. **WE** must resist the devil and our weapons are mighty to the "pulling down of strongholds." Even with the best weapons, it is still a fight.

RESIST MEANS FIGHT

Perhaps you agree with me up to this point, but feel that resist doesn't mean fight. In that case, ask one of our Viet Nam soldiers how they resist the Viet Cong. Suppose you're in command of our Da Nang Air Base when the enemy attacks. What would you tell your men to do. Resist? Right, but how?

Fight? You bet. With machine guns, mortars, grenades, flamethrowers and anything else that can be tossed into the battle. Your men will fight with all

they've got or be overrun. Don't let let Satan delude a single reader that resist means anything but fight. What's more, when an enemy gets too close for conventional weapons, the fighting becomes hand to hand combat. Our battle with Satan involves swords, shields, knives and bayonets. In close combat you can't tell the difference between the attackers and the defenders **by the way they fight.** It's to the death.

Satan must not be permitted to dampen our resistance with any thought that this is not a fierce fight. We need all the courage, weapons, strength and guts we can muster.

SUBMIT — RESIST

Here's another thing to note before we reach the actual technique for dealing with the devil. Looking at our text, we see there is another idea included which we haven't mentioned. Now we will. See it in the first half of the verse:

"Submit yourselves therefore to God"

After that comes, "resist the devil and he will flee from you." There's an order to observe. Also two different directions.

★ SUBMIT is GODWARD

★ RESIST is SATANWARD

One comes before the other. Why? The Christian who resists the devil must do so **in the Spirit.** Holy Spirit this time. By that I mean, one cannot think to approach Satan in the flesh and expect him to flee. That is laughable, for Satan controls the flesh. True, he does it by suggestion, but nonetheless he does it. He will not flee from our flesh. He likes it. He uses it. He lives there. Satan has no fear of us. Our weaknesses permit him to move us about like chessmen. To stand up to him **apart from Christ,** would only bring out his sense of humor. He would laugh like the Jolly Green Giant. It would be like an ant crawling atop the railroad tracks to tell a fast moving locomotive to stop!

 Submitting ourselves to God is humbling. Christians behave differently in the presence of God. They are meek, considering themselves sinners who owe a huge debt. They are joyful and peaceful, but never arrogant or rude. The man who would deal with Satan cannot approach him with a smart-aleck attitude. The moment he does, **he is in the flesh.** Rudeness and smartaleck talk are fleshly.

The man who pops off at Satan had better watch out. Retaliation can be swift. Satan is nobody to fool with. Christians must approach him with soberness. When Peter speaks of this, he says, **"Be sober, be vigilant . . ."** The Christian's attitude is one of caution, a self-regard which sees a man firm, poised, with dignity, even though he is addressing evil in person.

Remember how the archangel Michael, **"when contending with the devil . . . durst not bring a railing accusation against him"** (Jude 9), but brought the Lord's name into the conversation? Please note, however, that **he was contending.** There was a struggle. But no sarcasm fell from Michael's lips. Christians do not **rail** on Satan, even though they are the Sons of God. Why? The moment they try that, they are **no longer** in the Spirit. It is impossible to rail on some-

111

one and be in the Spirit at the same time. Railing is an act of the flesh. We're told to resist, not rail. **They are two different things.**

When you SUBMIT to someone, you put yourself under his control. This means we are to approach Satan under the influence of God's Spirit. We surrender ourselves to Him **first,** considering our helplessness apart from Him. To try and resist Satan without submission to God, invites defeat. By submission, I mean **conversation** with the Lord whereby we reaffirm our helplessness and lowliness a few seconds prior to resisting the devil.*

THE OTHER SIDE OF THE COIN

There are people who submit themselves to God, **but fail to resist the devil.** This is where most Christians are found helpless. They have no **knowledge** of the enemy. Even less have they any **faith** in his presence and power. Beyond that it has never occurred to them to **do anything about it.** For them, ignorance is dangerous. They are like the young girl who is devoted to her parents, but ignorant of boys. Her love for her parents doesn't protect her from the scheming lad who knows how to take advantage of female ignorance. **Sex ignorance** is dangerous in a parked car. **Satan ignorance** is dangerous in this hostile world.

It does little good to submit yourself to God, then fail to resist the devil. He flees only when resisted. Your conversations with God have no affect on him, but when you learn to resist him **personally,** the panic but-

---

*Is doing things IN THE SPIRIT new to you? The author's book, LONGING TO BE LOVED. can give you a lot of help. You'll learn how to close your eyes and instantly find yourself in the Lord's presence. And once there, you'll learn how to speak to Him and become so aware of Him, that you are powerfully fortified to confront your enemy.

ton is pressed in his headquarters. So we must always consider both sides of the coin. It is useless to resist Satan without first submitting to God. It is of no effect your submitting to God without resisting the devil.

DEVELOPING THE AWARENESS OF SATAN

It is only as we practice the presence of JESUS that we consider Him in our daily matters. When we are increasingly aware of His presence then we wonder what HE thinks of our words and actions. It is His presence that comforts us in trial, emboldens us in witnessing and makes the hardest of tasks seem joyous. So indeed, we practice His presence.

But the same applies to Satan. The more real he is to us, the more we watch for his hand. The greater our awareness of him, the more we guard our thought-life. The more intent our focus on him, the quicker we detect his working. Inasmuch as he lives to destroy us, we should be concerned with his presence.

When I was in India it was common to see the snake charmers displaying their craft in the street. They'd spread out blankets and line up the baskets of deadly cobras. When a crowd would gather, they'd uncover their treacherous pets and sound their flutes. The serpents rose from their wicker closets, swaying to the chant of their handlers. Did those snake charmers take their eyes from the cobras? Never! They focused on them, ready to move out of range the instant a snake decided to strike. A Christian can no more afford to take his eyes from Satan than a snake charmer can from his cobra.

● Dr. Norman Vincent Peale espoused the highly popular, **"Power of Positive Thinking."** The book you are reading is just the opposite. Since it is directed **against** the devil, it is more properly advocating the **power of**

113

negative thinking. The kind needed for victory. I want you to feel about Satan as the gazelle feels about a lion; or a rabbit the coyote. There is no room for positive thoughts about the devil. He is a killer, deadly, vicious — and FAST! Extremely fast! So — WATCH, watch, watch. Even before you pray. It takes but a flash to plant an idea in an unguarded mind. Buy one of his ideas and Satan has you.

Therefore an awareness of Satan is urgent for Christian victory. You may already find it hard to know the continual presence of the Lord and perhaps resent the idea of an additional burden. Believe it or not, discovering the presence of Satan can increase your awareness of Jesus. Can you see how the presence of our DELIVER-ER becomes more real as the presence of the ADVER-SARY becomes more frightening? It does, how it does!

TWO PEOPLE AT THE SAME TIME?

I hear the question in your mind. **"How can I concentrate on two people at the same time? Is it possible to practice the presence of Jesus and be aware of Satan at the same time?"** Yes. And it is easier than you suspect. In fact, you do it all the time.

Do you drive the freeway? Anyone who does, focuses on two things so **automatically** he isn't aware of it. (1.) He maintains proper control of his car. (2.) Keeps his eyes peeled for other cars on the road. A person must do both or he has no business on the freeway.

A driver must maintain the right speed, be ready with the brake and stay in his lane. Yet that isn't enough. He must also know where the other cars are and be ready for anything that develops. A sudden pileup in front and he has to be ready to swerve. You may not have noticed your focus on these two different things, but if you drive the freeway, you do them **automatically.**

114

Anyone who drives on the freeway must do two things automatically to keep from physical disaster. To have victory over Satan, you must do two things automatically — submit and resist — in order to avoid spiritual disaster.

● If you have never taken Satan seriously before, you must now. Think about him. Think of your life and what it could be in Christ. As you behold the gap that exists between what you are in Jesus today and what you would like to be, consider that much of it is due to Satan. That gap is enough to make you want to **do something about him.** If you can learn how to use your resources in Christ to deal with Satan, wouldn't you like to reduce that gap? Of course you would.

Nowhere in the book have I told you to resist temptation. I have spoken only of resisting the TEMPTER. Temptation is in a person. In the opening pages I reminded you that salvation was in a person. Consider now that temptation is also. When we see that the Christian life is a matter of our surrender either to Jesus or Satan, we reach the place where we can do something about it. From here on, the book deals solely with **WHAT TO DO ABOUT SATAN!**

CAUTION

If you are NOT a Christian, you will be unable to use this plan for SELF-DEFENSE against the devil. Until a man receives Christ as his Savior, he **belongs** to Satan. You may be able to resist temptation from time to time, but you cannot keep the devil from finally destroying your life. The devil will laugh at any attempts you make to use this plan. Without Christ in your heart, you lack the AUTHORITY to command Satan's departure, and you will have no permanent release of your life.

To become a Christian, you must deal directly with Christ. You must speak to Him as precisely as speaking to Satan has been set forth in this book. In a quiet moment, bow your head and talk to Him — like this:

 "Dear Lord, I know I am a sinner and that You alone can rescue me from Satan's kingdom. I desire to be with You in heaven rather than with Satan in hell forever. So I here and now open my heart to You. I ask You to come in and be my personal Savior. Amen."

If you can say that to Christ and mean it — He will come in — **instantly!** At once you'll sense you have been transferred from the devil's domain to the kingdom of Christ (Col. 1:13). A wonderful peace settles about your soul to certify the act has been done. After that, you may command Satan to depart whenever you feel his presence or pressure in your life!

PART TWO

Chapter Six

THE ANTI—SATAN DEFENSE SYSTEM

But Jesus said, "Begone, Satan! Scripture says, 'You shall do homage to the Lord your God and worship him alone.'" (Matt. 4.10 NEB)

In **SOUL-WINNING MADE EASY** my plan introduces Jesus as a living Person. Since He lives and is made real by the Holy Spirit, a Christian can **introduce Him** to someone else. The plan has four action steps. They are simple. They work. It is thinking of Jesus as a living Person, whom you can **introduce,** that keeps the soul-winning plan in mind. Think of Jesus as being present when you are talking to a prospect and you recall the plan at once.

Now Satan is alive. Just like Jesus. We must deal with him **person to person** also. Jesus lives to help us, Satan to hurt. Thus I want you to think of Satan as a PROWLER. See him as skulking about looking for ways to break into your **thought life.** Can you picture that? Good. This gives us a useful image as we unfold the plan for **dealing with him.** A plan that deals with Satan as a prowler can be kept in mind just as easily as one which introduces Jesus as a present Savior.

ANTI-PROWLER PROTECTION

A recent television show presented a home-protection expert. He had all the new devices for making a home burglar proof. He spoke of the growing concern in urban areas where rising crime rates are making homeowners jittery. He saw the day when widespread lawlessness would make it necessary for people to provide their own protection.

His display of gadgets interested me.

 First, he agreed with the Sheriff of Los Angeles County, who continually asks residents to leave a **light burning** in their homes when they go out for the evening. The expert had statistics to show that lighted homes enjoy a greatly reduced incidence of intrusion. Then he demonstrated light-triggering devices that could flood a person's yard with light automatically. He also had a bedside button which could turn on every light at once.

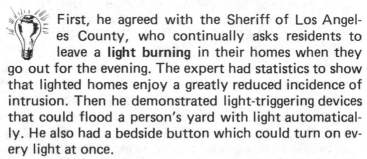 Next he showed **detection units** which wired fences and gates to a buzzer. Anyone coming over the wall or opening a gate, sounded a warn-

ing in your bedroom or a police station. He even had a means for letting you know when someone sliced a screen. His most sophisticated technique used TV cameras for monitoring every corner of the yards and doorways.

Then he brought out some **alarm bells** and gongs. Noise, he said, was effective against prowlers. I knew this to be true. A friend of mine had a dreadful alarm bell housed over his front porch. A button on the door casing let him keep his finger on it when answering the front door at night. Sure enough, a time came when he needed it. A surly intruder tried to force his way into the house and when the gong went off inches above his head, he nearly jumped out of his skin. That was the end of him. He fled down the street.

The last items displayed were **weapons.** He showed gas guns, electric shocking devices which were triggered by remote control, and unique holsters which fastened to your mattress. That way, if someone got into your bedroom before you detected him, you could reach a gun without making a suspicious move toward a pillow or night stand.

All of this was preparation for detecting and resisting an intruder.

Notice the order:

1. **Light**
2. **Detection**
3. **Alarm**
4. **Weapon**

Doesn't that suggest a scheme for defending our thought life against a spiritual intruder? If such things are effective for the protection of our homes, then their spiritual counterparts would surely be effective for the protection of our minds.

119

SPIRITUAL PROWLER

If we need LIGHT-DETECTION-ALARM-WEAPON to ward off the occasional prowler who comes near our house, how much more do we need that defense against someone who makes it his business to attack our thought life! We need just such a defense system. Our minds are more precious than our homes. Satan is an enemy worthy of the best defense we can devise.

Those four words:

LIGHT-DETECTION-ALARM-WEAPON

give us the basic defense plan. We have the equipment. God has already provided that. What we have lacked is a serious, **systematic way** of using it to resist the devil. But that sounds so simple, you say. Why not? Nothing God asks us to do is complicated. All it takes is willingness and determination. What I am presenting is a simple way to use what God has already given that we might have victory over Satan. When you behold the plan, you will be astonished at its simplicity. You will have the confidence to try it, because you can see God's hand in it.

THE DEFENSE SYSTEM

STEP ONE — LIGHT

Darkness invites the prowler. The Christian who gives no thought to Satan, grants him all the freedom he needs. When we say nothing about him, **we contribute to the blackout.** He has enjoyed obscurity all these years, because God's people have refused to take him seriously. Have you ever heard of a Sunday school class on Satan? Now that the evil hour is fast approaching, that must change. When his person and work become common knowledge and people start watching for him, serious limitations are placed on his operation.

The police use record systems to maintain vigil over the operational methods of criminals. A burglar who uses the same method repeatedly becomes known by his particular method. It is called his M.O., "Modus operandi," or method of operation. In many cases a criminal can be identified by the way he pulls a job, even when there are no clues or witnesses. If the pattern matches an MO on file, they have an idea as to who might have committed the crime.

Satan has an M.O. You've been studying it. You are acquiring **light** on the subject. As you **share** this knowledge with other Christians the light is turned up. When Sunday school classes begin to dig into this insight and **work with it,** the light gets brighter. When Satan's name creeps into Christian conversations, more shadows disappear. When God's people tell how they have **watched Satan flee,** it becomes a floodlight.

When preachers and teachers become serious about Satan and instruct their people, it's like the sun coming up. Satan hates daylight. He works at night. There are many things he just won't do with people watching him. As his techniques become common knowledge and Christians practiced in watching for him, much of his effectiveness is cancelled. We need that kind of victory today. It is important to share what the Lord can do for those who know how to deal with Satan.*

It does something for your own vigilance to speak of Satan. Drop his name now and then. Tell others how he works with suggestion, how he can plant ideas in our minds. Mention that he enjoys an access akin to that of the Holy Spirit. Anyone can see how he might dominate them with his appeals to weaknesses, appetites and ambitions. And when his ideas appear as our own, well . . . it's no wonder he's been getting away with it. We rip away his mask with that kind of talk. Will people ignore what you say? How can anyone ignore something he **sees at work in himself?**

Thus step one has to do with light. Light shed as we **learn** about Satan and **speak** against him. Did you ever think it could be as urgent to speak a word **against the devil** as it is to **speak for Jesus?** There are times when it can be. God's Spirit witnesses in both directions: His Word exalts Christ — it is also anti-Satan. The Holy Spirit certifies both truths. A Christian can minister either one — **in His might!**

STEP TWO — DETECTION

Here's where we apply Jesus' instruction . . ."**watch!**" Recall that we said, "Watching" **comes before** "praying." What do you watch? YOURSELF. Don't go peering into the air, you can't see the devil. If you want to look at something, **look in the mirror.** What will you see there? Yourself! That should remind you of his disguise

---

*If you find this plan has been a blessing in your life you might want to consider teaching a class on the anti-satan defense system. The author's book **TEACH THEM ABOUT SATAN** provides the know-how.

— SELF. Every suggestion Satan will bring is going to be dressed up in you!

● You have weaknesses. We all do. That's where Satan's attacks are concentrated. He strikes when trouble flares in one or more of your weak spots. Here's a list of common frailties. I use the general flow of the Apostle Paul's comments in Galatians 5:19-21 to establish the order. I am not suggesting one to be any worse than the other. You'll spot something you can identify as a weak area in your own life.

1. LUST. Your mind is triggered by stimuli. Frequently the imagination indulges in uncleanness. Since the hand simply executes something already taking place in the mind, God has no interest in location. Your imagination or a motel room appear the same to Him. Lust includes self-exalting dreams or any yearning to use others for self-gratification.

2. IDOLATRY. You are guilty of idolatry when you permit anything to come between you and the Lord. The usual order is family situations, overtime pay, a prestige position, or a week-end outing. Anything given priority over your obligation to Christ is idolatrous.

3. LAZINESS. Taking your ease at home? You know that the Great Commission calls each Christian. Tiredness, overwork, and other commitments employed as excuses for not investing yourself in some phase of the Lord's work.

4. TOUCHINESS. Resentment rises quickly when someone disagrees with you? Your feelings ignite when you are crossed by your mate, a child, or an employee? A difference in doctrine makes you resent a brother or sister in Christ? How do you react when you hear what someone has said about you?

5. JUDGMENTALISM. Measure others by yourself? "How that woman can let her children run around like

123

that is beyond me!" How quickly do you bang the gavel when others behave differently from you? Judgment can run from the way people dress to the places they go. Disapprove of speech, looks, cars, houses, vacations, the way others spend their money, run their churches and use their time?

6. FACTIOUSNESS. Do you divide at the drop of a hat? Are you like the deacon who rises at the church business meeting to declare the truth with vigor, but splits the church in the process? He's right in what he says, but wrong in saying it. Does unity have the priority in your thinking? Are you factious by insisting on an idea to the point of creating division? Will you spurn a working of the Lord because it bears the wrong label and divide over a minor matter of faith?

7. GOSSIP. "Probably I shouldn't say this, but you ought to know about it so you can pray for . . . " Such a thing is inspired in hell. Often it is done for the fiendish pleasure of passing along a degrading word. It is worse than any act of passion for it is not motivated by a drive of the body. Do you cloak your gossip in a spirit of piety?

8. WORRY. Anxious about the future? Social security? Insurance? Health? Bills? Family? Job? There is normal concern which moves us to careful planning. Overconcern mocks God's goodness. God has promised to meet every need. Any mental stress which suggests that God cannot handle your problem or overlooked something, is godless worry.

9. PESSIMISM. Negative feelings about life, church, the brethren? You are hard to please? Nothing ever suits you or is done to your satisfaction? You find it easy to complain about your job, mate, neighborhood, and the way things happen to you?

10. DOUBT. From time to time you wonder if the whole Christian program might not be one big fairy tale. Feel like you could be missing a great deal should faith turn out to be superstition only. Certain things about Christianity often seem incredulous.

11. SELFISHNESS. Usually the first in line. Want the biggest piece, closest parking space, best bargin in everything. Ignore the interest of others of the family. Stingy with Jesus.

12. DISTRACTION. Can't seem to focus on Christ. Hard to read the Bible and make sense out of it. Days fly by with nothing done. No definite plan for serving the Lord.

13. LYING. Get carried away when telling a story. Blow up the figures when speaking evangelistically. A little is always added to everything you tell.

14. DISSATISFIED. Restless at home. Feel that a change in jobs, neighborhood, or church is needed. Wish you could get away from it all for a while.

15. EASILY DISCOURAGED. Retreat at first sign of failure. Give up a plan easily, once it is overruled. Tend to quit when things turn out to be harder than you first supposed.

16. WASTEFULNESS. Squander the routine of life on yourself. Forfeit hours which could be used for spiritual preparation, devote nights to TV, putter with a hobby when Christian work beckons. Feel as though there is plenty of time to serve Christ in years ahead.

17. ABUSIVE. Weak temper control. Discipline your children severely when angered. Speak your mind regardless how it might affect others. Bawl out attendants who serve you publicly. Throw your weight around in public.

18. COVETOUS. Want things so badly you long to get them. Invest considerable energy in dreaming of things you see others enjoying. The mere sight of things you do not have makes you want them? So you enjoy them in your imagination.

19. DEPRESSION. Despair overtakes when you think of your problems. Life seems to be too much to face at times. Disappointments carry you into the depths. Deep moods overtake you at times. You feel like the walls are closing in.

20. FEARS. Afraid of the dark. Afraid of being assaulted. Afraid to speak out for Christ. Afraid of fire, death, loneliness, high places, sickness, etc. The awful stories appearing in the papers strike terror in your spirit. Sometimes you don't know what it is you fear. All you know is you're afraid.

21. PROCRASTINATION. Always mean to get involved with the deeper life and go all out in living for Christ. But somehow today isn't the day to start it. Down inside you know you should, perhaps even want to, but tomorrow appears better than right now. It seems too sudden to think of doing anything now. Consequently the moment of decision is deferred. You keep thinking that somehow it will be easier to execute it tomorrow than today.

Plus many more.

What I have shown doesn't begin to exhaust our spiritual disorders due to satanic influence. Many nervous and emotional aliments sending people to the doctors have their **origin** in Satan's hold on the Christian. I have mentioned these to show the extent to which he invades our lives.

SCAN THE LIST

126

I have not attempted an exposition of evils. Rather it is a hasty mention of some of the common weaknesses with the hope that you might be able to identify one you can see in your life. It will give us an item to work with if you can — a starting point.

I don't want you to study the list, just look at it. Besides picking an item which might fit you, observe that each has to do with . . . SELF! See that? Now consider the one you selected and ask yourself . . .

"Have I ever given Satan credit for that?"

Not likely. We don't credit Satan for the appearance of these things. The natural thing is to **blame ourselves.** We assume it is our doing since it comes from inside us. To blame Satan seems more like an excuse. He counts on that. That's what makes his disguise so perfect. But it just isn't so. You're going to be amazed at the part he has in the appearance of these evils once you know the joy of making him FLEE! You're going to be shocked at the way the pressure backs off when Satan's prodding is removed for a time.

I find that many of these evils appear in me. The pressures range from slight to severe. Nonetheless I can find nearly all of them in some measure. What am I doing about it? Concentrating on ONE AT A TIME. Experience shows me that it is better to focus on one weakness at a time. Which one? The worst one. Why? Because any **changes show up big.** Victory in your worst fault produces the most dramatic change in your life. You can put your finger on it. There is fantastic encouragement when you see yourself change. So your worst fault is the place to start.

SETTING THE TRAP

Now to lay a trap for Satan. Since he uses SELF as a disguise, the trap is really set for yourself. You will set up a watch over the **selected weak area.** The trap consists of a **continuous watch** over this area to notice the first attempt to indulge yourself. Of course, this will be new to you. So don't expect to catch Satan too early in the attack. You could be 5 or even 10 seconds into an attack before you suddenly awaken, **"Hey, wait a minute!"** That's all right for beginners. Later on you will be able to react the split-second a "fiery dart" hits your mind.

The hardest part of this four-step resistance is **detecting** Satan. Once you learn how to catch him in the act, it is a simple matter to deal with him. You can expect him to do all he can to keep you **from penetrating his disguise.** The last thing he wants is for you to become skilled in **recognizing** his role in your life. He knows what can be done in the power of Jesus' name once he is discovered. Therefore you can understand that learning to **focus on your weak areas** might not be as easy as it sounds.

Satan will do all sorts of things to move your mind from the target area. He can cause distracting interruptions. A difficulty may arise which will shift your mind from the weak area **to a problem.** If he is successful, your day will scarcely begin before he has you concerned about something **other than trapping him.** Should God permit it, you could go out of your house to find a flat tire on your car. That might be enough to make you forget Satan for a whole day.

● Learning to trap Satan is not easy. Therefore I have included some technique.

Let's say one of your weak areas is — WORRY. Lately you've been stewing about finances. Unexpected bills have you wondering how to make ends meet. It's been preying on your mind. You find yourself thinking about it much of the time. You purpose to work on this area seeking victory over it. You are ready to suspect Satan is using your financial situation to produce godless worry.

From your **Anti-Satan Kit**, select the card which reads . . .*

Satan says . . . WORRY
God says . . . "Be anxious for nothing, but in everything by prayer and supplication with thanksgiving let your requests be made known unto God. And the peace of God, which surpasses all understanding shall guard your hearts and minds in Christ Jesus" (Phil. 4:6,7).

"These anti-Satan weapons really help!"

*ANTI-SATAN KIT. This is a kit of 3x5 cards. I have prepared 17 of them which are to be used for the purpose of catching Satan in the act and dealing with him. On one side is Satan's suggestion concerning a weakness area and a Scriptural reply for putting him to flight. The reverse side offers mind-filling meditation to insulate your spirit against his immediate return.

Place the selected card on the dresser in your bedroom. It is ready to do a job for you.

Your trap is set first thing in the morning. You arise. You move toward your dresser and there is the card to remind you of the anti-Satan defense plan. Now it is on your mind. Instead of stewing about money, you will be thinking of what to do about the devil. As your fingers reach for the card, let that be a signal. Pause momentarily. Lift your spirit to Jesus. This is not special prayer, but a passing conversation that acknowledges His presence:

 "Lord Jesus, help me learn how to detect the devil's working in my life and to deal with him in Your name!"

Jesus hears you. He wants only to be asked and acknowledged.

Take the card with you to the bathroom. It's in your hand as you stand before the mirror. Look at the fellow in there. He's Satan's disguise. That's the guy you're going to watch. Now look at the card. "Satan says . . . WORRY ABOUT FINANCES." The weak area. Address yourself in the mirror:

"Satan will be after you today, ole buddy. He's going to work on that weak spot. The place I have to watch is your mind. He will try to keep your mind on the money problem. So I'm going to keep my eye on you. I'm asking the Holy Spirit to nudge me the first time the idea pops up."

That ridiculous sounding exercise adds enough weight to the matter to fix the trap. You've started something and the Holy Spirit will help keep it going.

Setting the trap for Satan!

Get dressed. Slip the 3x5 card into your plastic tract holder so that the "Satan says . . . God says," is showing through the back side. At the breakfast table, place the tract holder beside your plate. When you drive to work, put it on the dash where you can see it. At work, find a spot for it where you can see it, but away from the prying eyes of others. Think about it as your work ends and you return it to your shirt pocket. Take it out as you drive home and return it to the dashboard. Again, have it beside your plate at dinner. Put it on the night stand by your bed so that its message is before you as you retire. You can expect Satan to attack at night.

Sound melodramatic? It is. Remember you are shifting from a life of no Satan watching, to one that sets traps for him. Naturally everything is a little hammy at first. So you overact, so what? The significant thing is that you are on guard. You will catch him. Why? Because you are alert and watching. When you get used to it, Satan-watching becomes as natural as breathing, as normal as prayer.

131

PLUNK

Some traps sound like that. When I was a boy, we used to make traps. We'd prop a box on a stick with a string that led away to our hiding place. A trail of grain would bait a pigeon or dove under the box. Then we'd pull the string and "plunk." The box would fall on the quarry and we'd have him. It was exciting to **wait** and **watch**.

Our Satan trap is like that. That's why you are watching. The bait is your financial problem. You're waiting for him to show up with his suggestion. Day after day he's been plaguing you with worry. Now you're ready for him.

When did it happen? The instant he thought your mind was unguarded and he could bring on the suggestion. Let's say you've returned home from work. Dinner isn't ready yet and you've gone into the den. Wouldn't you know it. The mailman brought another bill and there it was on top of your desk. That did it. **"Another bill! Man alive, I'll never pull out. What am I going to do?"** You can feel a bill, hold it in your hands and read the amount. It's got to be paid. The very sight of one can trigger emotion when you are already buried under a pile of them. Satan counts on that.

"Bills, bills, bills. I'll never get ahead. Wonder if I can borrow..."

OH OH

The Holy Spirit nudges. You suddenly remember **"Satan's here!"** You almost shout it. You've caught him. Yank on the string. That unleashed concern over bills was his doing. The trap is sprung. Worry did move into your mind, but now you're **thinking about Satan.**

132

He's in your trap. You can deal with him. And when you do, watch that worry flee with him!

See how it works? When you find yourself involved with the weakness and suddenly your mind moves to Satan, aware that this is precisely how he works . . . **the trap is sprung.** That's the trap, you see. Being conscious of him in the same moment you find yourself indulging in the weakness. Putting the weakness and Satan together is the whole point of the number two step. If you can bring yourself to think of the devil the moment a weakness strikes, you've got him. From there on the power of the Holy Spirit makes the task easy. **Detecting the devil** is the hardest part of our defense system.

Watch out! Satan can use those bills!

INSTANT SUCCESS?

No. When you first start to use this method, you won't catch yourself right away. More than likely you'll drift deep into a weakness before it occurs to you, "Satan's doing that." But that is only because it is

new. The more you work with it, the quicker you catch on. Every time you detect the devil, it will be because the Holy spirit has nudged you. We can depend on Him for that. That's His part. We do our best to be Satan-conscious, but even with our best efforts we don't succeed apart from the Holy Spirit's gentle touch.

Most of our weaknesses are so powerful they **blind.** Take jealousy for example. The jealous person is consumed with this emotion the instant it is triggered. Since the emotion itself is overwhelming, how likely is that one to think of Satan? Not likely at all. Therefore it requires the Holy Spirit to do something to help. Take the one who boasts. Bragging words swell inside and escape his lips. He is so carried away with what he is saying, he is not about to turn his mind toward Satan **without help.** No, dear reader, this plan depends on the Holy Spirit's willingness to help us. Without Him, our minds would never focus on the enemy.

● I mention this so that you may consider how utterly this plan **depends** on the Holy Spirit. When does the Holy Spirit nudge? He sounds His warning the instant Satan strikes. It isn't loud. Quite faint in fact. Far from overpowering. But it is enough to be an alert signal. The secret is **conditioning ourselves** to hear it. Obviously, when we are first learning to use the resistance plan, we're clumsy. We're not used to listening for the Spirit's call. When we finally get it, Satan has had our weakness in operation for some time. Our sensitivity increases with use.

I selected financial worry for our illustration since it is so common. But it could have been worry over ill health, your job, or your children. Worry can be a disease, like jealousy or lying. It is more than a habit. It is a weakness which Satan turns into sickness. The only remedy is **dealing** with our enemy who has such power.

And you are ready to do that. **You've caught him.** He has triggered financial worry by the sight of a newly arrived bill. He's not going to get away with it this time.

STEP THREE — THE ALARM SOUNDS!

Suppose it is a dark night when you come sneaking over my back fence. You're treading your way very stealthily across the yard, certain that no one has seen you. But I've been watching. I see you. Suddenly I call out . . . "Bill!" You'd jump out of your skin! You thought you were getting away with this sneak-entrance, then . . . DISCOVERED! It's a shattering experience to have your name called out in such a moment. I don't suppose you have ever been through a thing like that, but I have. It's devastating.

Satan moves in darkness satisfied that his SELF disguise is working as usual. All of a sudden . . . "SATAN!" You call his name. It's not enough that you have penetrated his disguise, but to hear his name like that is a **shock treatment.** Step three is a shock treatment for Satan.

SPEAK TO SATAN?

"Brother Lovett, do you mean I am to talk to the devil?"

Yes. Absolutely. I alluded to this earlier, but you probably didn't know quite how I meant it. Now there'll be no mistake. I want you to **talk to Satan.** And do it as definitely as you talk to Jesus. Talking to Jesus is prayer. Talking to Satan is our resistance. Whether to Jesus in prayer or to Satan in resistance, it is the talking that gets the job done.

This is the ALARM in our anti-Satan defense system.

SCARY

Does the thought of addressing the devil leave you cold? It might. It's one thing to say, "Speak of the devil," when someone shows up. It's quite another to talk to him **in person.** To speak to someone of such rank, higher than the President of the United States, and give him a direct order isn't a casual thing. Christians can make light of the devil in a happy group. But facing him alone, after you've found yourself a **sinning victim,** isn't so funny. The first experience of working up enough courage to speak to the "god of this world," can give you the shakes.

I remember the first time I spoke directly to Satan. I told you about it in Chapter Three. Oh, did I feel shaky that first time. I spoke and then waited, wondering if he would hit me. I expected the ceiling to fall in. But it didn't. You can take advantage of my experience. I tell you now, Satan will not do anything to you. So you can be more at ease about this than I was.

Mine is not the only experience which can give you counsel. Is the name Theodore Epp familiar to you? His "Back to the Bible" broadcasts are well known. He has traveled this same route. His testimony could add assurance.

"For a number of years I felt those pressures. At times I had to get in my car and drive into the country for talks with God to get any relief. Then one day I realized such pressures had to be coming from Satan. God gave me discernment to see that satanic forces were depressing my mind in an effort to control me. I found the way to victory in the

Word. For the past year or two it has not been necessary for me to go into the country to get rid of pressures. You can resist Satan and be an overcomer at all times." *

Dear friend, I tell you now, you will suffer **no retaliation** for dealing with the devil. But I guarantee also, that he won't go away unless **you tell him to.**

WHAT DO I SAY?

Calling out Satan's name is but the first word of our resistance. After that comes **your command** to him . . . "GO!" You see, we are not left on our own as to what to say to Satan. Our Lord Jesus set the pattern. The Scripture is clear. Our Savior met the devil in His wilderness testing and dealt with him. While it was a genuine testing for our Master, it is also an example for us. We can hardly go wrong following the example of our Lord Jesus:

"SATAN! BEGONE! FOR IT IS WRITTEN . . ."
(Bible quote)

There it is. We can't expect to improve on something our Lord Jesus used when HE dealt with Satan. The success of this method is recorded too, "Then the devil left Him."**

SATAN A DEFEATED ENEMY

This is a glorious truth. It is part of our working knowledge. But at the same time many Christians are **misled** by it. Some feel Satan has no real power over them because our Lord Jesus met him in contest and defeated him; that the victory of Christ over Satan somehow makes us immune to his evil thrusts. **Nothing could be further from the truth.**

---

*"Nervous Christians," Dr. L. Gilbert Little (Moody Press). p. 122.** Matthew 4:10,11.

"Satan! Begone! For it is written . . . "

Yes, Satan is defeated, praise God. But he is not dead. Neither is his strength diluted. He is just as powerful as ever and as deadly. He is just as ready to fight. He has never yet been defeated by a Christian. Satan has not an ounce of fear of any man. He can do almost any thing he wants with you and me. We have no strength to match his. For us to challenge Satan to a fight would be a joke.

Jesus defeated him. He does fear Christ. And he truly dreads the name of Jesus. He hears the One in Whose name we speak, not us. The very sound of our Savior's name must be awful to Satan. When it is spoken to him directly it stabs his memory. Five letters J-E-S-U-S carry him back to the cross where he was openly whipped in his own blunder. What an agonizing reminder that name must be! It must be a little like the way a former boxing champion feels when someone mentions the person who took his crown.

The name of Jesus is our AUTHORITY for speaking directly to Satan, even as it is our authority for approaching God and making requests. Again and again our Lord tells us what we can do in His name. So much so that the Apostle Paul enjoins:

 "Whatsoever you do in word or deed, do all in the name of the Lord Jesus . . ." (Col. 3:17).

Resisting Satan is no exception. I submit the very mention of Jesus' holy name is a shock for the unholy spirit. How the evil one must cover his ears, humanly speaking, when that name is uttered **against him.** My imagination sees him shrinking and bruised when we resist him in the Victor's name!

The power of a name

 The famous banker, Baron Von Rothschild, was visited by a young businessman seeking a loan. He had come highly recommended, but the shrewd

139

Rothschild saw that the application didn't warrant the loan. Turned down, the young man was crestfallen. His hopes were shattered.

The Baron's heart went out to him. He rose from his chair and escorted him through the outer offices taking him personally to the front door of the building. There he put his arm about him and consoled him with . . .

"You are going out of here with something better than the money you wanted and it hasn't cost you a cent."

Of course, the young man saw only failure in his visit to the banker. He had no idea what the wiley Rothschild meant by his remark — until the next day!

Cards from industrial leaders began to arrive. Businessmen dropped by to see him . Offers were extended to him. The money world was interested in someone who appeared to enjoy the confidence of the mighty Rothschild. Scores of businessmen had seen the Baron's arm around the young man. The name of Rothschild rubbed off. So that's what was worth more than money — **that powerful name!**

The name of Jesus has more than rubbed off on us. We wear it. That name is to us what a uniform is to a policeman. Whenever he wears it, his acts are authorized by the department. When he pounds on a door, he says, **"Open in the name of the Law!"** His own name is never mentioned. In fact, he wouldn't dare try such a thing in his own name. No one would pay any attention to him if he did. He has authority only as he speaks in the name of the Law!

When we resist Satan **in the name of Jesus,** we are in uniform. When a Christian stands up to Satan in Christ the enemy sees JESUS! When we speak in that

140

name it is as though Jesus is saying "BEGONE!" This is why we humble ourselves before God first . . . to put on the uniform.

We all cringe at the sight of some uniforms!

You can see how any attempt to resist Satan **out of uniform** would be ridiculous. We are then resisting him in OUR OWN NAME. He has no fear of us. Only Jesus does he fear. Even the angels are cautious of the mighty Satan. So you can see I am not suggesting a glib approach to our enemy. It is only as we are conscious of our **personal weakness** and **utter dependence** on Jesus' name, that we dare such a thing. It is a **reverent act of faith** to use this POWER OF ATTORNEY. It is done in meekness. It is too precious to be handled any other way.

Therefore I have added . . . "IN JESUS' NAME"

. . . to our resistance. Doing so accomplishes two things. First, it reminds us that our name is ineffective and forbids any arrogant blast from us. Also, the mention of Jesus' name is like an **alarm** clanging above his head. While we are comforted by it, Satan is shattered by it. He is startled. He looks. He beholds the UNIFORM and the AUTHORITY that goes with it. **That's what makes Satan cringe.**

When Satan beholds Christ **in our resistance,** he sees the one who defeated him. When we use that name in our resistance, Satan's defeat comes before him. Until **we speak** in the name of Jesus, Satan's defeat does not apply to the Christian. There is no automatic victory. Any more than there is such a thing as automatic prayer. We must speak to God in Jesus' name. We must also speak to Satan in that name before the victory of Christ goes into operation. Remember, it is like my garage door. That powerful motor waits to do its work, but nothing happens **until I press the button.** The victory of Christ is like that.

So now what does our resistance look like?

"SATAN! IN THE NAME OF JESUS, GO! . . . (quote)."

What yet remains of our defense system? The weapon. The thing that really drives Satan away. Here it is.

STEP FOUR — THE WEAPON

"Is not my Word like as a fire, saith the Lord? And like a hammer that breaketh the rock into pieces!" (Jer 23:29).

God's Word is described as "The Sword of the Spirit," or a weapon. It is the **only offensive** equipment listed in the armor of Ephesians Six. It is our solitary means of **countering** satanic suggestion. When an ungodly notion arrives in our minds, it amounts to . . . "SATAN SAYS." The only counter is what . . . "GOD SAYS!"

So many of us take comfort in God's Word and receive instruction from it, we just don't think of it as a weapon. But we'd better. It's the only thing we have that is effective against Satan. Perhaps this is the first time you have taken a serious look at the Bible as an anti-Satan cannon. I trust it will be God's encouragement to take up arms against the enemy.

ANTI-SATAN WEAPON

Do you believe in the supernatural character of God's Word? I'm sure you do.

Did you know that the Holy Spirit is able to anoint His truth to any heart — **Satan's included?** By anoint, I mean explode the reality of it. Perhaps this is even more true in the case of the devil, since his appreciation for the Word is greater than ours. With him, it is not a matter of believing the Bible to be the Word of God, he knows it. He was there when it was written. He watched the authors pen the lines; saw the spiritual operation which provided the inspiration. This is why we read, "the devils also believe and tremble" (James 2:19).

The devil **trembles** at the Word of God! What do you think of that? It is some weapon that makes your enemy tremble. The enemies of the United States no longer quake at the awesome might of our atomic arsenal. They have one too. But Satan has nothing to match Scripture in the hands of God's people.

What is it that makes Satan fear the Bible? Is it the

fact that millions of them are in print? No. Does it bother him when Christians study the Bible? No. Is he pained when they quote Scripture passages in their gatherings and sermons? Indeed not. The Scriptures by themselves don't affect Satan. He knows the Bible by heart and can quote chapter upon chapter. He's so clever with the Word, he can design subtle twists in it for his agents. He enjoys distorting the Word so that it becomes his tool, instead of God's. That's fun for him. There's only one time when Satan fears the Word of God . . . WHEN IT IS USED AGAINST HIM!

When the Bible is used as a WEAPON **against** Satan, he shudders under the impact of it. When a Christian SPEAKS the Word of God to Satan, the Holy Spirit moves into action. Something amazing happens which smashes the power of Satan and crumbles his spirit.

Soldiers and weapons

Let's say that back in the late 60's you watched our boys in Viet Nam as they sat cleaning their weapons. One studied his carbine and thrilled with the ingenious design. Another put a high polish on his .45 automatic. Another saw how fast he could set up a machine gun. As the men studied and practiced with their weapons, did the communists flee? That's funny. What enemy ever fled because someone else examined and practiced with his weapons? See the point?

Bible study doesn't make Satan flee. If you were under attack from the enemy and took out your Bible to read, he wouldn't be impressed. **Bible drills don't make Satan run.** You could memorize the Bible from Genesis to Revelation and recite verses hour upon end, and he wouldn't shy from you. He'd join you and first thing you know, you'd **feel proud** of your accomplishment. He can be present in a study class and not a word will bother him. Why? Because none of it is **directed against** him. None carries the explosive might of the Holy Spir-

144

it, because none is addressed to him **personally** in the name of Jesus. That's what makes the difference.

Have you ever emerged from a darkened auditorium into broad daylight? Your hand flew to protect your eyes. I remember a biology class where we darkened the room to study slides. In time the bell rang and we rushed outside. My eyes were immediately struck by the light. I felt great pain. It hurt so badly, I can recall it as I write these lines. The pain has lingered in my memory for years.

"The entrance of Thy words giveth light. . ." (Psa. 119:130); **"Thy word is a lamp unto my feet and a light unto my path. . ."** (Vs.105).

God's Word, used as a weapon in the hands of His saints, is a flashbulb fired in Satan's eyes. There is pain. And since darkness and light cannot remain together, **he must flee.** This is the Christian's strength against the devil, the floodlight of God's Word shining in Satan's eyes! The thing to notice, though, is that it must be turned toward him. It has to be used **as a weapon** against him. It has no anti-satan force until the Christian speaks that Word in Jesus' name.

The next time you have an attack of worry, depression or doubt, try quoting Scripture verses to yourself. Hours later you'll still be suffering. Why? They are aimed in the **wrong direction.** Turn them toward the devil, in Jesus' name, and the miracle happens. The difference between practicing with a weapon and firing it is obvious. One act amuses the enemy, the other scares him away.

SPIRITUAL SIX-GUN

In frontier days, our forefathers went about with six-guns strapped to their waists. The absence of any

 law made it necessary for each man to provide his own protection. It would have been fatal for those with this world's goods to be without some means of defense. Covetous men didn't hesitate to kill for gold. Frequently a man's life depended on the speed with which he could produce his weapon and fire.

Your spiritual safety is no less dependent on your ability to produce God's weapon **and fire.** It isn't strapped to your side, neither is it carried about in a pocket. That's too slow. This weapon has to be on the **tip of your tongue.** Yes, I am saying that you must arm yourself with anti-Satan verses. God's Word has choice replies for **every** suggestion the devil can offer. You must have them ready for instant use. As soon as Satan's suggestion hits, you go into action.

SATAN SAYS	GOD SAYS
WORRY	"Be anxious for nothing."
GOSSIP	"Love one another, bear one another's burdens."
COVET	"Set your affections on things above."
LUST	"Be ye holy for I am Holy!"
BE DISSATISFIED	"Be content with such things as ye have."
FEAR	"My peace I give unto you. . ."
DEFEAT	"Be of good cheer, I have overcome the world."

You can see I am not talking about Scripture memorization for its own sake. But if you memorize verses which have to do with your weakness areas, the Holy Spirit can bring them up as soon as Satan strikes. That gives you a "fast gun!" It is a thrilling experience to see how quickly Satan flees when God's Word is fired at him. The pressure release comes at once. That's a different use of God's Word. You can understand how any weapon is ineffective until used. All that I have said here in Step Four is summed up in the idea of **USING GOD'S WORD AGAINST SATAN.** I realize it has other uses in the life of a Christian. We're talking about it as a **WEAPON** now. For that is its function with reference to the devil.

A WORKABLE SYSTEM

Here is our basic scheme for resisting Satan.

LIGHT	DETECTION	ALARM	WEAPON
(Insight)	(Watch weakness)	(Speak to him)	(Use God's Word)

The graphic image of an intruder trying to gain access to your thought life helps to keep the plan in mind. We have a vicious, undercover enemy who knows all the tricks. He can get an idea into our minds before we realize it. Unless we have a defense system which is alert and ready to retaliate, he will get away with it. It's obvious that this knowledge is vital to Christian growth. Christian victory is impossible without it.

The system in review

1. LIGHT

This book sheds light on Satan's operation. More light is shed on him as you speak of him:

a. Talking to God about him, makes you more Satan-conscious. This makes it possible for the Holy Spirit to show you the devil's working in your life.

b. Talking to others about him, turns on the light for them. This sharing of insight alerts them to his working and makes it possible for them to have victory also. God is pleased when we share the good things He reveals.

147

c. Talking to yourself about Satan, heightens your watchfulness. Talk to yourself about your weaknesses. See how honest you can be. The more open you are about them, the easier it is to recognize Satan's attempts to use them.

2. DETECTION

We set a trap for Satan by establishing a watch over our worst weakness, or the one in which we indulge the most often. We must be honest with ourselves about this weakness so as to increase our sensitivity. As we are about to become involved in it, or find ourselves beginning to become involved, the Holy Spirit gives a "nudge." A voice within says, "SATAN!" At once we shift our minds to the devil. The trap is sprung when we catch ourselves in a weakness and think of the devil at the same time. We have then penetrated his disguise to deal with him while he is at work. If we delay, it is too late.

3. ALARM

Having caught Satan in the act, we're ready to press the alarm button. Instantly we lift our spirit to God speaking first to Him, so as to be conscious of our sinful state. This removes any temptation to resist the devil in our own name. Then we SPEAK DIRECTLY to Satan as did the Lord. His example tells us what to say . . .

"Satan! Begone! For it is written . . .(verse)!"

I have added the NAME of Jesus since we are told to do all things in His name. Doing so reminds us that our name is useless. We are humbled by this, but that humbling is also our strength. Christians are mightier in meekness than in arrogance. Commanding Satan to . . . "GO!" . . . in Jesus' name INVOKES THE DEFEAT he suffered at Calvary.

4. WEAPON

The Word of God is a supernatural weapon. Satan dreads its

148

power only when it is used against him. The storing of Scripture verses, which counter Satan's suggestions for our weaknesses, provides the child of God with supernatural ammunition. The verses directed against the devil IN JESUS' NAME become blinding flashes. Satan, who is darkness, must flee before the light of God's Word.

IT SOUNDS SIMPLE, BUT OH DOES IT WORK!

GODLY CHRISTIANS VULNERABLE?

How about the man who lives close to the Lord, is he vulnerable? Is that Christian who spends much time in the Word and almost fully occupied serving, also vulnerable? Yes, he is. To the same extent? Yes. Then you mean preachers and missionaries are also open to satanic suggestion? Indeed I do.

The more serious a person becomes about Christ, the higher becomes Satan's desperation to thwart him. The more determined a man is to invest himself in Jesus, the more furiously Satan tries to keep him from it. It is often true that men closest to the Lord suffer the strongest attacks. Was not our Lord under continual assault even to the cross? Yet He lived as close to the Father as one can get. His devotion to obedience did not make Him immune to Satan. Nor will it any man.

However the man of God may not always be toppled by the same wiles used on the **carnal** Christian. He has to be reached with loftier and more noble suggestions. Pastors, for example, could not be led into gambling or the reading of cheap novels. But church programs, budgets and ministerial gatherings can beguile them. Consider the pastor who is led to feel that success in the ministry means a large building and congregation. He is highly vulnerable to any satanic suggestion for furthering this noble ambition.

I know of one who had a very adequate building. He really wasn't doing much with the congregation he had, but he longed for a larger one. Somehow he became convinced that a nice new building would attract crowds and fill the place. He thought an appealing building would draw people more readily than the Gospel. And he was right. There are lots of people who can be attracted to a building, who are indifferent to the Word of God. And that was the trap.

He got the plan approved through the sheer force of his personality and position as pastor. The building was erected, but the burden of it fell on a few families. There is now a huge debt which will last for years and years. The emphasis of the church shifted. The appeals have gone from Jesus to dollars, for the financial load pinches. Many in the congregation are weary of being asked for money. Yet the begging must continue for a long time.

This pastor was deceived by a good thing. A new church building is a good thing under the right circumstances. There are many good things Satan can use to snare sincere Christians. There are moments in the lives of the godly when Satan's suggestions sound great. When that happens, the man without a defense plan is helpless. **Godliness is no defense against the devil.** He must be resisted and that requires action — SATAN-WARD!

DON'T GET MAD

It is natural to spit out something that tastes bitter. What I have just said might infuriate a person in a similar position. But please don't get angry. You can see what I am trying to do. I just want to help.

 Consider the Indian who was invited to look through a microscope and see all the germs which lived in his drinking water from the Ganges river.

He was told not to drink that water any more, that it was deadly. He looked. When he saw all the wiggling germs, he took a heavy club and smashed the microscope and continued to drink the water.

Now you can ignore this book, throw it away or burn it and remain indifferent to the truth of satanic suggestion and how to deal with it. But that won't change the fact. If year after year goes by without any significant changes in your life, you can be sure of Satan's dominion over you. Therefore, one of the most urgent things you can consider is a **workable** defense plan. I offer that **dramatic** victory in the Christian life is **almost** impossible without it.

We sing, "Faith is the victory that overcomes the world." Your faith cannot become that kind of victory until you believe what God says in His Word.

Try the plan I have set forth. It really is simple and it costs you nothing. Once you sample the **flight** of the devil, it will be a turning point in your life.

Wait and see!

Chapter Seven

USING THE PLAN!

"Submit yourselves, then, to God. Resist the devil, and he will flee from you." (James 4:7 NIV)

"Do you think it is wrong for a Christian to learn the art of self-defense?" inquired a ministerial student of his pastor.

"Certainly not," was the answer. **"I've learned it and use it all the time!"**

"You do!" The youth was astonished. "Did you take up boxing or Judo?"

"Neither. I learned the James system."

"The James system?"

"Yes. You'll find it in the 7th verse of the 4th chapter of the book of James. 'Resist the devil and he will flee from you!' That's the best system of self-defense I know."

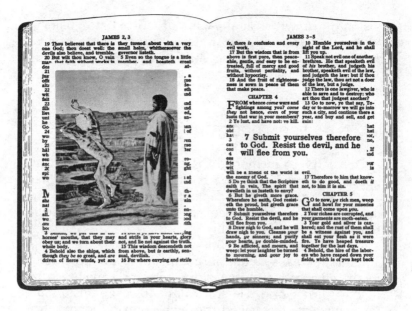

NO SHORT CUT

There is no quick, easy way to learn how to **fight**. It doesn't matter whether it is boxing, wrestling, combat training or resisting the devil. You have to work at it. It takes time to develop a skill. And that means practice, patience and serious work outs.

I would deceive you if I led you to believe that Satan-resisting was a grace you could acquire instantly. Reading this book will no more make you an accomplished resister, than hearing a lecture will make you a polished soul-winner. This skill is gained as you **work with it**. It takes practice and experimentation. The more seriously you apply yourself, the sharper you get.

When you begin using the defense system, your legs will be wobbly. You are entering new, unexplored territory. That always makes for uneasiness. Strange little apprehensions accompany the first attempts to speak directly to the living devil. But isn't that also true of visitation or witnessing? A lot of "first time" fears go with any new work we undertake for Christ. And remember that you will be shifting from doctrine to action. There is a strangeness about that too. Often a surprise.

FROM DOCTRINE TO ACTION

Don't try to memorize the doctrinal material in this book. You need only the basic truths of Satan. When you have absorbed this general sense, you have all the doctrinal preparation needed for resisting the devil. Here they are in a nutshell:

1. Satan, perhaps second in command to the Lord Jesus in the days of his former glory, remains a mighty ruler in the spirit world. He still rules and maintains a separate kingdom. The fall corrupted his great wisdom, turning it to craft and guile, but none of his power is lost. It was diverted from the glory of God to satanic self interest. God is presently using the tremendous investment He made in Satan as a means of producing a race of TESTED citizens. Satan will be banished forever when the earthly program is concluded (Rev. 20:10).

2. Satan BECAME the "god of this world," when Adam rebelled against the will of God. He joined the DISOBEYERS of whom Satan was already chief. Man's dominion of the earth passed to Satan's hands that day. Subsequently, every child of Adam is born under satanic control. Christians are delivered out of it by the miracle of the new birth which translates them into the family of God (Col. 1:13). This gives Christians a dual status. Part of them is under the control of Satan and part of them is under the control of Christ.

3. The new birth equips the Christian with a new nature (New Man). That part of him is under the control of the Holy Spirit. The old nature, (Old Man) which remains

154

until physical death, is under the control of Satan. The Christian is like a third party, FREE TO CHOOSE which nature he will manfest. He does not have to serve the old nature if he doesn't want to. This is God's way of DELIVERING Christians from the POWER of Satan. Whichever nature the Christian chooses to obey, determines whether he will live for Christ or the devil. It is the struggle between the Christian's two natures that makes for spiritual growth.

4. The Spirit of God and the spirit of Satan have **equal access** to the UNCONSCIOUS portion of our minds. They can quicken material already on deposit or that which is newly arriving by the senses and send it into the thought-life in the form of a SUGGESTION. Man is free to respond to these suggestions or refuse them. Therefore, it is the Christian's responsibility TO DE-CIDE whether the Holy Spirit or the unholy spirit will dominate his life.

5. The spirit of man (old nature) and the spirit of Satan are identical in function. When Satan triggers an idea in the unconscious, it arrives in the thought-life AS THE CHRISTIAN'S OWN. Since it has to do with himself, he does not suspect an outsider has had anything to do with it. Satan does not plant ideas that exalt Satan. No Christian would worship him. In heathen lands he can inspire devil worship, but in Christian lands his aim is to get Christians to live FOR THEMSELVES rather than Jesus. This is how he strikes back at Christ Who defeated him at Calvary.

6. Satan controls the Christian by bombarding the thought-life with suggestions which appeal to SELF interest. SELF is the disguise for satanic activity in the Christian's mind. The disguise is so effective, Satan is never credited with the waste and evil found in the average Christian. Satan succeeds because his ideas appeal to the Christian's passions, instincts, appetites, and

natural ambitions. When a man lives completely for self, he is filled with the unholy spirit. When he lives completely for Jesus, he is filled with the Holy Spirit. A person can study his own life pattern to determine how much of him is under satanic control. The extent to which he lives for himself is the measure of his FILLING OF THE UNHOLY SPIRIT.

7. Christians have been cautioned by the Lord to WATCH for Satan. If a Christian can catch the devil at work by detecting satanic pressure on a weakness, he can resist him. The New Testament describes the Christian life as a warfare. The singular strategy for meeting Satan in conflict is our Lord's example during His wilderness testings.

● If you can absorb these basic truths, you are doctrinally ready to deal with the devil. From this point, all you need is a plan for doing it. I have taken the:

1. **WATCHFULNESS** enjoined by our Lord (Matt. 26:41);

2. **RESOURCES & WEAPON** cited by Paul (Eph. 6:14-17);

3. **RESISTANCE** counseled by James and Peter (James 4:7, 1 Peter 5:8-9);

and woven them into a simple defense system. It is fashioned after the idea of protecting one's home against a prowler or intruder. The thought life of the Christian is the battlefield inasmuch, "As a man thinketh so is he." Control a man's thinking and you control the man. This is what Satan is after. Therefore, defending your thought life against satanic suggestion is the best way to "Resist the devil!" Tremendous victories for Christ can be won by installing and using this defense system. Here it is again:

			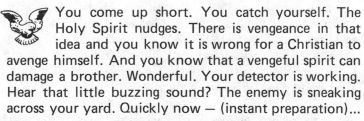
LIGHT	**DETECTION**	**ALARM**	**WEAPON**
(Insight into satanic operation.)	(Watching over a weakness.)	(Speak to God, then to Satan in Jesus' name.)	(Use God's Word to counter Satan's suggestion.)

IN ACTION

The mailman has just brought a letter. It's from a company seeking confidential comments about a job candidate. They learned that you knew the applicant in days past and are eager for your evaluation. What they don't know is that the man caused you considerable trouble and discomfort. Your pen is ready. You are about to answer.

Does Satan have any suggestions? You bet. How do you think they will arrive in your thought life? Watch your mind return to the former trouble. Satan can stir the sordid details in your unconscious and send them to your imagination. You recall the scenes and the unpleasant feelings return. Satan counts on these feelings to motivate a hostile report. Then he strikes: **"I thought the day would come when that guy would be sorry."** Ah, did you hear Satan? No. You heard yourself. See the disguise? That was Satan speaking — **as yourself.**

 You come up short. You catch yourself. The Holy Spirit nudges. There is vengeance in that idea and you know it is wrong for a Christian to avenge himself. And you know that a vengeful spirit can damage a brother. Wonderful. Your detector is working. Hear that little buzzing sound? The enemy is sneaking across your yard. Quickly now — (instant preparation)...

"Lord Jesus, forgive me for entertaining any hint of vengeance in my heart and help me to resist the evil one . . ."

THEN . . . "SATAN!"

That startles him. But didn't he hear what you just said to Jesus? Yes. But conversations with Jesus don't bother him. Now your words are **aimed** at him. You call his name. It shakes him. Rarely does anyone ever do that, but you just did. A sense of horror enters his being.

"IN THE NAME OF THE LORD JESUS!"

He covers his ears. That dreaded name. What's worse, something is coming toward him in that name. Something is being leveled straight at him. Satan can be made to shudder. The host of evil trembles when that sacred name is used against the prince of evil.

Satan is no longer thinking about your old wounds and how to hurt you. He is thinking of the cross. He trembles as he recalls the fierce might of his conqueror — the LORD JESUS! Instead of your wounds, his old wounds produce feelings in him. The hour of his defeat returns. That name repeats the agony of his own ruin. Satan feels awful. Now to use his feelings in that name.

"GO AWAY! BEGONE!"

The devil does a double-take. He stares at you. What does he see? The UNIFORM of the Mighty God who "bruised his head," at Calvary! No weak, puny human is ordering him. That UNIFORM of Jesus' name gives authority to the command. It's like seeing a flashing red light in the car mirror, there is no choice. You have to stop. Mild panic grips your heart.

Satan reacts against **you** for giving that command? No. That uniform is official. It represents the One Who is mightier than he. To retaliate against you for ordering him away, would be like fighting with Jesus. He's already been defeated by the Lord. That victory is relived the instant you speak to him in Jesus' name.

"FOR IT IS WRITTEN . . ." The offensive weapon is drawn and fired:

 "Avenge not yourselves," says the Lord, **"vengeance is mine. I will repay"** (Romans 12:19).

There. It is done. What do you feel? The first thing is relaxation. The inclination to use the "confidential report" as a means for vengeance is gone. In its place is a desire to please God with what you put on that paper. Your mind goes to Jesus. You sense it could be a thrill to do what HE wants right now. Sure the man abused you in the past, but what is that? Before you is the opportunity to bring pleasure to the One Who died for you. When Satan backs off, your mind quickly moves to do that which is pleasing to God.

There is rejoicing in your spirit as you fill out the form. It was a miracle. It occurs to you that it was fun to put Satan to flight. And even more of a delight to do that which is good in the sight of the Lord. The Savior is pleased. You feel it. The Holy Spirit has a suggestion which enters your mind . . .

"Well done, thou good and faithful servant."

That, dear reader, is sweet!

POWER IN A FORMULA?

What is it that makes our resistance formula work so well? Is there magic in the words to make Satan panic? Certainly not. However, it appears on the surface that an ordinary Christian has uttered words which made the mighty prince flee. If it is not the formula he uses, what is it?

Answering that uncovers a missing doctrine. For some reason it has been ignored, that action on our part **begets action** on the part of God. This truth is not taught any more. Maybe I have put it clumsily. If so, let me restate it as the . . .

"YOU GO FIRST" CONCEPT

If you are an active witness for Jesus, you already know how this works. You speak a few words to a prospect and WHAM! It is as though you pushed a button and the machinery of heaven went to work. With little effort on your part, the prospect feels the conviction of sin, senses the reality of Christ and knows He is needed as Savior. What is it that accomplishes this? Your words? No, the **power of the Holy Spirit.**

But you did have to speak. The Lord waits for the Christian to open his mouth. He speaks first. Then the power of God FOLLOWS. That's the YOU GO FIRST CONCEPT. It has ever been this way. Did not the Master give the order, "GO YE into all the world . . . and I'LL GO WITH YOU!" See? **We go first.** We speak, He moves. We open our mouths and the Holy Spirit anoints our words. That's the power, anointed words.

The Christian addresses a few words to Satan in Jesus' name and the Holy Spirit goes into action. He explodes the Word in the heart of Satan, just as He does in a lost soul. But see this; no words, no power. No action by the Christian, no action by the Holy Spirit. I illustrated this earlier with the button which raises my garage door. I push and there is power. If I don't push there is no power. Thus our formula is simply a means to help us GO FIRST. Then God does the real work before our eyes!

A push! And there is power!

Door rises in the power of the motor!

GETTING STARTED

1 Select a weakness in your Christian life. Go over the list in chapter six and see if an area doesn't hit close to home. Pick one. It will be enough for you to set up the watch over one area. We all have more than one weakness, but I am anxious for you to catch him in the act just one time. After that you will be hooked. Victory tastes good. You'll want more victories. I am satisfied that once you enjoy the thrill of his flight, you'll be sold on the idea of a defense system.

> **WEAKNESS:** Suppose you choose procrastination. You are a Sunday school teacher and for some reason, always seem to have something to do besides preparing for Sunday. You suspect Satan might be responsible. You enjoy teaching, but "more important" things seem to interfere with your preparation.

2 Set up a watch over your weakness. If you have a built-in procrastination tendency, Satan knows about it. He can deceive you with the thought **"There's plenty of time."** If you buy it, it won't be hard for him to get you to defer your work until the last minute. Then it might be too late. Now to catch him at it. Install the detection technique.

a. On a 3 x 5 anti-Satan card it reads . . .
   SATAN SAYS: "Wait until later. You have all week to get ready."

   GOD SAYS: "Redeem the time" (Eph. 5:16).

b. Insert the card in the clear, plastic tract holder with the face showing. Place it on your dresser so that you will spot it first thing in the morning. When you awaken, take it with you to the bathroom for the mirror exercise. Study the face you behold, to remind yourself that Satan wears a clever disguise . . . YOU! His attack will come in the form of a thought which appears to be entirely your own. Naturally, it will appeal to your flesh and your weakness in some way.

162

c. As you behold SELF in the mirror, glance at the card in your hand. Arm yourself with the Scriptural counter to Satan's suggestion. Have the verse on the tip of your tongue. Talk to yourself about it:

"I know Satan's suggestion is going to be one which will get me to put off preparing my lesson for next Sunday. I will answer him with God's Word which instructs me to do my work heartily as unto Him. It is impossible for me to be a hearty worker and a procrastinator at the same time."

Getting ready to use that verse against Satan!

d. Have the card conveniently in sight as you do your housework. Or, if you report to a job daily, find a place about your desk where it can serve as a remind-

163

er. When you return it to your purse, that can be a further signal to your mind. As you drive home you could be thinking about a time when you might go to work on the lesson. Pick it up as you leave the car and go into the house. Place it at some strategic point where you will see it in the course of your normal movements about the house. It is not a reminder that you have a job to do, but one which says, "Watch for the enemy!" At this point, we're interested in catching him in the act.

> NOTE: Beginners seldom detect the presence of Satan until they are pretty well involved in the thing he has engineered. But don't be upset with yourself if you find that you have forgotten about him and fail to think of him until long after he has maneuvered you into an evil situation. This is normal for those learning to watch for him.

❸ A few days go by. It is possible a working lady would have things to do which might keep her from getting the lesson ready early in the week. But now it's Thursday night. No meetings, no shopping schedule. Ah, it seems so good not to have to do anything. Your hand finds the TV guide. Oh, the "Thursday Night Movie" looks good. Sounds like a comedy. Fine for relaxing when someone's had a full day.

"Besides, I have until Saturday night to get my Sunday school lesson ready."

POW! Your eyes catch sight of the plastic holder and its message. The weakness. Those words, "You have until Saturday night." Whose were they? And do they sound like a hearty worker of the Lord? The moment has come. You sense the sound of satanic inspiration. There's no doubt that the suggestion appeals to your flesh. Relaxation and entertainment appeal to a woman at the end of a busy day. Here then is a definite event.

You can put your finger on something that might well have its source in the devil. Ready to try resisting him? Good for you.

4 This is done privately. Go into the bedroom and even out into the garage if you want to. The bathroom is a good place because the mirror reminds of the disguise. You might swallow hard. Maybe your voice cracks at the first words. You feel apprehensive? Sure. There's a whopping difference between theory and practice. But you're going to try anyway:

"SATAN, IN THE NAME OF THE LORD JESUS, GO! GO AWAY! FOR IT IS WRITTEN, "Redeem the time . . ."

There now. That wasn't so bad. The ceiling didn't fall in did it? Of course not. But you felt timid. That's all right. Christians are stronger when they MOVE in meekness. God's strength is made perfect at just such a time. Don't ever feel that shyness gives Satan any advantage over you. It doesn't. The opposite is true. If you have the shakes, they are but "first time" fears. Next time will be easier.

5 Results? Satan leaves. What do you feel? Walk back into the living room and see. Look at the TV. Still think you want to watch that movie? No. A new suggestion comes to mind. It can be very thrilling to let the Holy Spirit show you some new things about the Sunday school lesson. In fact, you find yourself looking forward to sitting down to the lesson. More than that, a strange new motive sweeps over you. You want to do it just to please the Lord. You're thinking about Him now. And doing what HE wants seems even more appealing than watching the TV.

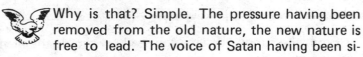Why is that? Simple. The pressure having been removed from the old nature, the new nature is free to lead. The voice of Satan having been si-

lenced, the voice of the Holy Spirit rings clearly in your soul. When the one who has power over your flesh is ordered away, the One Who dwells in your new nature can have His way. You find yourself thinking about the Lord and what you might do to please Him. No longer is it an obligation you must carry out, but a delight and a privilege. Your excitement mounts as you begin to obey. Within moments you find more entertainment and relaxation out of doing the will of God than you would watching TV. That miracle occurs **when Satan flees.** But had you not ordered him away, you would never have tasted such a joy. This kind of victory is glorious!

Satan lost that round!

IT ISN'T HARD

From the supposed case, you see how simple the plan

166

is. What the Sunday school teacher did in watching over her procrastination weakness, someone else could do with any weakness. Selecting the cards, using the mirror exercise and having the countering verse ready for Satan is about all there is to it. Once you catch him, or even suspect him to be at work, you can speak to him using the Word of God in Jesus' name! The Holy Spirit takes it from there. He is the One Who makes it easy.

The **results** depend entirely on how seriously you take God's Word and stand in faith as you speak to Satan. Putting on the UNIFORM is not simply a matter of adding Jesus' name to the phrase, but an awareness that there is nothing in you from which Satan would flee. If you truly speak to him in Christ, he'll flee. Don't worry about that. He doesn't want that Word anointed to his heart. He hates its bright flash. The sight of your uniform strikes terror to his cowardly spirit. He'll flee. There's nothing else for him to do.

When he does flee, you can thrill to the wonder of it. It is a miracle. Be ready to thank the Lord with all your heart. It is His working, His victory, His Spirit that did it all. The few words from your lips, simply set the POWER OF GOD into motion. All you did was push a button.

AN ACTUAL CASE

A friend of mine, a former officer in a corporation, was served with a subpoena. A national airline was bringing suit against his old corporation, seeking to have the barrier removed. They wanted to collect damages from the officers as individuals. There was a huge bill and now the airline was taking legal action.

My friend reacted as might anyone. He had no responsibility in creating the bill. But he was an officer of the corporation at the time the bill was incurred. The airline, should it be successful in setting aside the corporate barrier, would be able to collect part of the debt from him personally. It was unjust, but it does happen and he was faced with the threat of it.

How would Satan use this? Worry. My friend really had something to worry about. You could almost say it was a "legitimate" worry. Of course, there really isn't such a thing, but we can't help being human at times. So he took the problem to bed with him. He tossed with it all night and it was his companion throughout the next day. And the day after that, and the day after that. By the time I got a chance to talk to him about Satan's role in such a thing, he had a pretty good case of anxiety going.

I laid out the steps just like you find them in these chapters. Since we were talking face to face I was able to make sure he understood the plan. He was determined to try it. And, of course, I was eager to hear how he made out. He called the next day:

"Well, brother, I tried it, but I don't think it did much good. Maybe it works differently for me than for you."

"Are you going to give up or try again?"

"Oh, I'm going to try again. It may be just a matter of my faith in Satan. After all, this is pretty new to me. But if there is victory here, I want it. Honestly, brother, I'm desperate."

That's what I wanted to hear. I knew it might not be easy to go from one conversation with me to another conversation with the devil and do it with the same faith by which he was used to approaching God. In fact, I didn't see how he could possible have enough faith in Satan (God's Word actually), to deal with him as he would with the Lord. So that's where we spent the rest of the discussion. He began to get the idea.

"Bill, you're familiar with the verse, 'Ye have not, because ye ask not,' aren't you?"

"Sure."

"Well, the same thing applies to victory over Satan. 'Ye have not, because ye resist not.' Our resistance to Satan is just as definite a step as petitioning God."

"But I did resist him, I think."

"Bill, have you ever noticed in prayer, that when you mean business, you pray out loud. When the situation is really serious you get down on your knees. And finally when you are truly desperate, you cry out to God with the tears streaming down your face!"

"I've done that."

"Well, it's the same with the devil. If you really are serious about victory in your life, you'll deal with him in no uncertain way. You'll talk right up to him. You'll command him. You'll stand in the name of Jesus and with full authority order him to leave. When Satan is as real to you as Jesus, you'll deal with him as urgently as when you're on your knees before God! Understand what I'm saying?"

"I get you."

I waited for Bill's next report. I was sure his strength would develop. At least the first time fears would be behind him. He waited a few days before calling me. I was getting a little anxious. But his words eased everything . . .

"This thing is really great. I don't think Christians have any idea of the power of Satan."

"Tell me about it, Bill, how did it go? Last time we talked you had doubts about the plan."

"The first couple of times I don't think I did any good at all. But last night, I told the Lord that if there is anything to this business of resisting the devil, to help me or I was going to forget it. Then I just out and told Satan I didn't want anything to do with him and he might as well take off. You know what? He did. I guess I finally meant it."

Bill's words didn't exactly fit the formula, but they contained the one thing needed for Satan's flight. He spoke to Satan without any doubt as to his presence. He spoke in faith. You can see what that does. It doesn't matter whether we are asking of God or telling Satan to go, it is the **lack of doubt** that makes the difference.

FROM DOCTRINE TO ACTION

Expect early failures. Did you know that Thomas Edison had 10,000 failures before he finally invented the electric light bulb? But who remembers them? His one success was so great nobody ever mentions the discouragements he faced. Failures mean nothing when success finally comes. Each one simply brings a person that much nearer his goal.

I'm not saying that you will have 10,000 failures, or even ten. But you might have six or seven. The first time you speak out against him and tell him to go away, it may only make him laugh. It could be that your mind is so **full of doubt** about him and the power of God's word to dispel him, it simply amuses him. Without meaning to, you will be resisting him **in your own name.** But don't let that bother you. The Master knows we have to learn this skill, even as we learn any other Christian task. He will protect you. Satan will not be allowed to retaliate. When your heart is set to live for the Savior and do

His will, you can't get hurt. And each failure will bring you closer to success.

Your doubts provide the biggest barrier at first. "Does Satan really hear me?" "Does he really go away when God's Word is directed toward him?" Can the Holy Spirit use the Word as a sword against the devil?" Perhaps I'm just talking into the air?" "I feel so foolish doing this!" Such thoughts flood your spirit at the beginning. You will feel awkward and foolish. Remember the first time you talked aloud to the Lord? It wasn't any different. It took getting used to. But in time you did it. Now you don't think anything about the fact that Jesus is unseen.

It's like that to address an unseen person by faith. It isn't easy. Your first attempts will be **experiments** and that's fine. In time, resisting Satan will be **as natural as talking to Jesus.** All you need is one success and it will do as much for your defense system as your first answered request did for your prayer-life. Success has its own way of wiping out all discouragement. So be prepared for several failures before you taste success. Once you taste the thrill of having Satan flee, you'll agree that WATCHING can be as important as PRAYING (Mt. 26:41).

BREAKING BAD HABITS

Sometimes a Christian is bound with a bad habit. He longs to be delivered, he yearns to be free. He agonizes in prayer, yet still feels guilty before God. The more he prays, the tighter seem the chains that bind him. And he remains in this bondage until a traumatic accident of life fills him with an over-powering determination to change. Or he can try the Bible's way — resisting Satan.

This same Christian can be set free by **dealing directly** with Satan. He can speak to the devil using God's word in the power of Jesus' name and the pressure eases at once. The same formula can deliver a Christian from any habit, whether drinking, stealing, smoking or sexual abuse.

The difference between dealing with a habit and suggestion is that the **suggestion** can be removed in a **one time dealing with Satan, the deliverance from a habit requires a long drawn out** fight. Habits, as you know, do not occur overnight. They are developed over a period of time. Hence their solution is not instantaneous either. It might be necessary to order Satan away a hundred times the first day of the battle.

The intensity of the habit determines the intensity of the fight. Satan does not give up easily with a habit, since he enjoys the power it gives him. You are vulnerable continually and he can manipulate you almost at will. He enjoys mocking God through you and delights in the guilts that compound inside you. So he will not let go easily. He has to flee the moment he is ordered, but he lurks just out of sight. The next unguarded moment, he rushes in. And the process is repeated.

Habits are BUILT through **use.** They are BROKEN through **disuse.** The disuse comes as you resist Satan over a period of time. Let a habit be abandoned for several weeks, even though it means a steady fight, and you'll find that most of the fire has gone out of it. This is how the victory is won. But like any victory, it requires a fight. Yet this is the kind that can be had through the power of God's Word. And it can be had anytime the Christian really wants it.

But notice this. There can be no victory of this sort, until the Christian **does something about Satan.** Satan is the source — he must be dealt with.

REPLACING SUGGESTIONS

Most of our victories are not a matter of breaking

deep-seated habits, but resisting the tempting offers Satan presents to our minds. When they are spurned, they have to be replaced. The devil's suggestions are to be replaced with God's suggestions.

When Satan flees, your mind is free from his suggestion for a time. What will you do with your mind, now? If you don't want him to come back with another suggestion, then it must be replaced with another's. Whose? God's. It is one thing to be released from the tempting power of Satan's suggestions, it is something else to replace them with God's Word. **The sweetest changes occur in the Christian life when we allow God's suggestions to replace Satan's.** The best way to discipline your mind is to take heed to God's suggestions.

 "Wherewithal shall a young man cleanse his way?" asks God's Spirit. **"By taking heed thereto according to Thy Word!"** (Psa. 119: 9).

See how this works. When Satan backs off at your command, the Holy Spirit can rush a replacing thought to your heart **if you make it possible.** I have found that memorizing verses which **matched** my weakness not only gave me ammunition for the time of Satan's attacks, but also provided mindfilling ideas which could **replace** Satan's suggestions. The Word of God is a TWO-EDGED sword. One edge does its work in Satan's heart, the other edge does its work **in mine.** The same verse which I use to resist Satan is also full of rich things which can change my life.

HOW IT WORKS FOR ME

 The other day I saw a brand new station wagon. The color was my favorite and everything about it suited my choice in cars. Of course, it was expensive. I knew there was no way to spend such a sum just for a car, but that didn't keep me from **COVETING**.

Oh, oh, a weakness showed up. It was easy enough to get the thought out of my mind, but the weakness didn't go with it. Satan backed off at once, but he didn't take my covetous spirit with him. I hadn't considered covetousness as a personal weakness before. Now I **would**. I had been alerted and would prepare for attacks.

The Mirror-Method works in a car too!

I selected the proper card from the anti-Satan kit Personal Christianity has developed:

174

SATAN SAYS ... COVET

GOD SAYS . . . "Delight thyself also in the Lord and He will
give thee the desires of thine heart."

I took a moment to have a little talk with the man in
the mirror. I wanted him to see himself in that verse. I
asked, "What does that verse mean to you, my friend?"
I wanted him to break it down for me!

1. "Delight thyself." You looked at the station wagon and
thought it would bring you great delight to have one like
it. The idea of having one brought pleasure and satisfaction
to your soul. You were thinking how you might "delight
yourself." So you know what that means, don't you?
Yes, I do.

2. "In the Lord." Oh, oh. That means to have the same
passion when you look at Him and the job He's given you.
Yes, but can a man have every one of his yearnings
satisfied by the Lord Jesus? That's an honest question,
man in the mirror. What is the rest of that verse?

3. "And He will give thee the desires of thine heart."
Free—with no monthly payments. I see what you mean. If
I shift my focus to finding all of my pleasure in Christ,
then He Himself becomes my pleasure. So that's how He
satisfies me! If all my longings are for Him, then I can be
fully satisfied. Since He is an INFINITE SATISFIER, I
can know the satisfaction 10 station wagons couldn't
match!

Does that little scene sound ridiculous? Perhaps. But
you can see what I was doing. This was more than a
Scripture memorization exercise. I was fitting the understanding of that verse to the need in my life. Then when
I next used it to dispel a satanic attack of covetousness,
it would do more than flash in his face. It would also fill
my mind with suggestions about the One Who alone can
satisfy me.

That is a terrific help. It guarantees that **no mental**

void exists when Satan flees. Besides, it adds to my growth in the Lord. God's Word has a supernatural power which can build us as we understand it. The Apostle Paul was aware of this:

"**And now brethren, I commend you to God and the Word of His grace, which is able to BUILD YOU UP and give you an inheritance among all them that are sanctified**" (Acts 20:32).

This is particularly true when I store verses to **match my weaknesses.** You've heard the formula for success in the world, "Find a need and fill it." Well, the same is true of God's Word. When a verse meets a particular need, its effect on your life is mighty. When you consider that the same verse can also be used as an anti-Satan weapon, you acquire a new appreciation for its power.

I have found that a single verse which not only rids me of the devil, but fills my mind with God's suggestion, possesses a supernatural **keeping power.** The Holy Spirit can send those suggestions to my mind and after Satan has fled **they** will control me.

HERE'S HOW IT WORKS

A pretty, new secretary was assigned to your office that day. She was a shapely dainty and every time she walked past your desk the devil was able to bring you under attack. While you wanted no part of it, you sensed a vulnerability to unclean thoughts. Now you are at home. You are determined to maintain a clean mind for the Holy Spirit.

You select a verse for your defense system:

"**Be ye holy for I the Lord your God am holy!**"

That's a great verse. It has the tender element of, "Like Father, like son." We do want to be like our Father in heaven. After all, we're going to live with Him forever and the more like Him we are, the sweeter the relationship. You have a few minutes before dinner, so you talk about it to the man in the mirror.

Some spiritual refreshment before dinner.

Dinner's over. You are seated before the television set. The plot brought the attractive heroine to the place where she is helpless before the hero. We always identify with the hero. You are in the story, too. That's why people watch TV, to get involved. That lovely girl, strangely reminding you of the new girl at the office, is in a compromising position. She needs your help.

"Help me. I'll do anything you say. Anything!"

Satan moves! He has a suggestion about that "Anything." The board of censors would never allow the story to develop on the screen as it unfolds in your imagination. Within seconds a sordid solution to her problem takes shape in your mind. The juicy scene is unwinding when . . . "Buzzzzzz." A nudge from God's Spirit. You are a **Satan-conscious** Christian. The detector is working. You've caught him in the act!

177

"The Enemy!" You exclaim. "Oh, Lord, he got me that time. Forgive me and help me to resist him!"

God hears. You move. Now . . .

SATAN! GO! In the name of JESUS, GO AWAY! For God says . . . "Be ye holy, for I the Lord your God am holy!"

You made a quick draw. Satan flees! You know you were under attack, for now the pressure is gone. You feel the release which follows his flight. But you know he'll come back. Perhaps you change the channel. Maybe you leave the room. But regardless, you don't want unclean thoughts in your imagination. Your mind moves again to the verse. This time the Holy Spirit uses it to strengthen you. He answers your meditation. His suggestions fill your mind.

"If holiness is going to be my future home, I might as well get used to living a holy life right now. There's no point in indulging myself in even the tiniest bit of lust, if there is not going to be any of that stuff in heaven. I'd better start learning how to enjoy holiness right now."

"It is only reasonable that a man cannot learn to be holy overnight. If I am planning on being as holy as God, I'd better get with it this minute. I'm learning about it right now. In fact, this experience with the TV can be an important step in my holiness program. And I am sure that God is pleased to think that I really do want to be just like Him!"

When the Holy Spirit leads a man to conclusions like that, you can be sure a supernatural work has been wrought in his heart. Natural man does not think like that. Meditate on your verse in that fashion and you'll almost thank Satan for his attack. It has been the means of turning your mind to one of the greatest truths a Christian can know. Now see what has happened. An evil situation has been turned to the glory of God. That's victory my friend, real victory.

VICTORY

This book has provided enough biblical insight for you to take Satan seriously. It has outlined a simple defense system for safeguarding your thought life. This is the real target of satanic attack. The resistance formula has already been demonstrated to be effective. It was our Lord's defense in His wilderness testings and I have found it miraculously true in my own life. I have given you the plan in the clearest, simplest language I know.

You may have to practice a few times before you taste the flight of the devil, but everything needed is here. You may have "tongue in cheek" as you read now, but a moment will come when you will be desperate for deliverance. Then the Holy Spirit will use this material to help you deal with the evil one. Once you taste the thrill of having him flee, your life will never be the same.

Also, the flight of Satan makes it possible for you to lay hold of God's Word in a wonderful new way. His Word has the power to change you into the likeness of Christ, but that can't happen until its truth dominates your mind to the same extent as Satan's self-centered suggestions.

Even though we live in a world of temptation, every attack of Satan can be **stepping stone** to maturity. Once you experience the way this know-how releases you from Satan's grasp, weaknesses in your life can be eliminated by the miraculous power of God's Word! Until you enjoy that release, you will never taste a major victory.

After you read the book, Satan will have a sugges-

179

tion . . . "I don't need that. My life is so dedicated to Jesus, Satan couldn't have any real influence. Besides, my whole life revolves around Christ."

DON'T YOU BELIEVE IT!

Ask yourself this?

"Would I like to enter heaven the way I am right now? And stay that way forever?" If not, you will have to get serious about Satan. He's in the plan of God, too. If you are spending your time, money and energies on yourself and **your family** to the neglect of God's call, you are in the "snare of the devil." If the routine of your living permits one day after another to pass without your doing anything to advance the cause of Christ, it's time to **recover yourself** from that snare.

God says, **"Be ye Holy . . ."** — NOW! Right now, not just in the life to come. Can you say, "I am as holy as Jesus in all my ways. My life exudes His holiness in everything I do and say? His perfection is found in every corner of my imagination, every movement of my hands and every word from my lips? I have reached the fullest maturity this life can produce?"

Can you say that and be satisfied it is true?

No? Why not? Why aren't you that way? Is it because you don't want to? That can't be true. Every child of God yearns to be like Jesus. It hurts him to think that he is far from being what he ought to be. The answer lies in the fact that SOMEONE ELSE has a hand in our lives. Satan lives to keep us from being what we should in Christ and he is successful at it. May God grant you the grace to change while you still have time.

PUT SATAN BEHIND YOU!

Does all you have read sound overwhelming? Really it

isn't. It's just new. The first time you saw the multiplication table, you said, "Do I have to learn all that?" Now you use it automatically. Was it any different when you started to drive? Once you knew how, there was nothing to it. And so it is with resisting the devil.

Won't you take one weakness, one area and work with it? See if you don't become alert to Satan. You'll find you can catch him in the act. Then don't be afraid to speak to him in Jesus' name. You'll thrill to the power of God's Word as it does its work before your eyes. And the name of Jesus will become more precious than ever.

With all this focus on Satan, I don't mean for you to take your eyes from Jesus. When you drive your car, you don't focus on the brakes. You watch the road. Yet you make sure the brakes are working properly. If you suspect they could be faulty, then you do think about them — plenty. That's how I want you to regard this anti-Satan defense plan. If it is working properly, then you can forget Satan. You'll use the plan just like you use the brakes on your car — **instinctively.**

Our main objective is to stay close to Jesus and be mindful of His indwelling presence. When your defense system is working as it should, it brings you **even closer** to the Lord. His Word captures your mind and you have days filled with His presence. You see changes in yourself as you become more like Him. That's what you want, isn't it? Of course.

This book was written to help you do it!

181

Appendix

Some Questions . . .

After Reading "DEALING WITH THE DEVIL?"

1 "In the book you say, 'Forget demonology.' Is this because demons are somehow unreal or unimportant?"

ANSWER: They are real, they are important. Their afflicting presence is found in many lives. My reason for asking you to forget them is that we might focus on Satanology. This book deals with the devil, not with demons. I felt it would be a contribution to separate these activities. Satanology and demonology should be treated as **SEPARATE SCIENCES** for they have a very basic difference:

Satanology is concerned with **RESISTING ATTACKS** against one's own person.
Demonology is concerned with **CASTING OUT** beings already lodged in someone else.

Resisting attacks against one's self and casting beings out of another are obviously very different matters. Thus they should be separated and approached differently. Each requires a skill quite different from the other. Unfortunately many today confuse Satanology with demonology. Mention the devil and their minds picture demon possession. This simply is not valid. Satanic attacks must be REPULSED, while demons have to be DISLODGED. Repelling and dislodging are very different works. I trust this difference is obvious simply by mentioning it.

In the Gospels the demoniacs (those occupied or controled by demons) are consistently viewed as HELPLESS VICTIMS. In every case the demons are ALREADY LODGED and in control. This is not so when a person is under attack, for then Satan is TRYING TO GAIN control. The N.T. examples are already victims of the demons. They are not regarded as evildoers or conscious wrongdoers, but as SICK PEOPLE. Consequently, demonology is a matter of treating the sick, those with pathological conditions. Satanology is for those who are well, and provides the means whereby people can avoid this kind of sickness. It is obvious that most Christians fall into this category.

The title of this book is **"Dealing with the Devil"** NOT "Dealing with the Demons." That could be the title of another work. I have purposely and deliberately isolated the skill of SELF-DEFENSE against Satan from that of CASTING OUT demons already lodged in others. The anti-Satan skill is easy, quickly learned. It can be used the moment one reads the book. But the casting out of demons is hard. It is not risky, but requires fantastic faith. A few good men in this country have such a ministry. They find it hard. The results they achieve are nowhere near what they long to see. On the other hand, even children can be taught to resist the devil. There is no danger and they can experience wondrous results the same hour.

It is good for Christians to learn of demonology, but I would hope that every reader of this book will make the distinction between it and Satanology.

2 "Are many in America demon-possessed today?"

ANSWER: Only the tiniest portion of the population. Most are in mental institutions. Why? They have to be. Demon-possession means demon-control. And demons are by nature destructive, bitter, vicious, hateful and cruel. Individuals under their control are dangerous. They menace society. They have to be confined. The chief characteristic of a demon-possessed person is the extreme damage he does to himself and others.

Insanity and epilepsy appear to accompany the N.T. cases. Consequently it is possible to diagnose demon-possessed people as psychotics. However they can be distinguished from other types of mental illness by the strange aura about them. They seem almost unreal, and well they might, for citizens of another world indwell them. A person who has finally submitted his will to demons, so that they (or he) exercise complete control over him, is a machine of destruction. Even so, note the demoniac of Gadara. Though he had so many demons, still they were not able to kill him, or get him to kill himself (Mark 5:1-20).

Demon-possession is NOT common in the U.S. It is more prevalent in the lands of ignorance and superstition. Why is this so? Americans acknowledge the FACT of God. If they were to involve themselves deliberately with any spirit-being, HE would be the one. But in lands where people worship that which frightens them, their superstition leads them into WORSHIP STATES, which in turn make them easy victims for Satan. Satan makes the conquest, he invades the person. Then his demons are left to occupy and hold the conquest for him. Startl-

ing cases have been reported by missionaries and investigators in foreign lands.*

Keep in mind that Satan can produce mental and
physical illness BY SUGGESTION, and that much of
what is called demon-possession, is not. There is no possession at all, just damage and sickness. Possession requires a **surrender** of the will, but sickness requires only an **approval** by the will. Many of God's people suffer
sicknesses, serious ones, but they are not demon-pos
sessed. They are victims of satanic suggestion. While the
actual number of cases of demon-possession is very low,
perhaps less than 1/10th of 1%, the number of people
who suffer sickness due to satanic suggestion is high . . .
perhaps 80% of the population. Doctors readily admit
that most of the cases coming to them have no organic
cause.

3 "Can Satan attack a Christian's body by direct assault?"

ANSWER: No. He is not allowed to touch us, except as
he can stir others to act against us. Herod's slaughter of
the infants was of this order, as you recall. And in the
case of Job it was a matter of very special permission
(Job 2:6). He is a spirit-being and consequently limited
to the spirit realm. His power is limited to suggestion.
Our thought-life (imagination) is the meeting point of
these two realms. Even so, suggestions whether from the
Holy Spirit or the unholy spirit have to be approved by
OUR WILLS. This is why permissiveness must precede
possession.

Should we buy any of Satan's suggestions, THEY can

---

*Moody Press has a paperback edition of "Demon Experiences in
Many Lands." This could add to your store of knowledge on this
fascinating subject and perhaps aid in your discerning the difference between the damage done by satanic attack and that which
occurs through actual possession.

hurt us. Not only as they lead us into evil, but they can also damage us physically. **Illness can be produced by suggestion.** Great forces exist within the human mind. It is estimated man uses less than 5% of his mental capacity. Most of our body functions are unconsciously controlled by the AUTONOMIC NERVOUS SYSTEM. Breathing, blinking, circulation, muscle movements and most all organs are directed by this system, which is in turn directed by the unconscious mental control center.

Throw a crippling idea in that center and the damage can appear in the body. Some of Satan's ideas we DO ACCEPT. And it is by permission that much of the damage we suffer occurs. He cannot hurt us unless we permit it, but alas we are easy victims for many of his suggestions. They appeal to our passions and weaknesses, likes and dislikes. We are vulnerable. Some of his suggestions do real damage within the psyche, manifesting themselves in the body. I can't expand on that here, but we are pushovers for the devil until we learn HOW he uses our natural desires to exploit our frailties. Few suspect the evil they tolerate in their thinking can produce sickness in their bodies. But it is true, man is a product of his thinking.

This is why we must set our "affections on things above" (Col. 3:2). Why Paul says, "Whatsoever things are true, lovely, pure, honest, etc . . . think on these things" (Phil. 4:8). It is not enough to tell Satan to go, we must also keep our minds busy with that which makes for mental health. The healthiest thing I know is to live moment by moment in fellowship with Jesus.

Again, there is nothing to fear in terms of physical attack from the devil. He is not allowed to cross into the physical so as to afflict us in the flesh. But as you can see, neither does he have to. We must guard our hearts and minds, for that is the area of damage, spiritual and physical.

4 "You didn't say too much about the armor of Ephesians Six. Do you feel such weapons are unimportant in our war with Satan?"

ANSWER: Indeed not. They are indispensable. Countless expositions have been made upon these verses, yet another word might be said. The most urgent fact concerning these weapons, i.e., faith, truth, righteousness, etc. is that this equipment is all **MENTAL.** It is one thing to regard the Roman soldier's battle-dress and make nice applications, but quite another to behold these weapons as needed for the believer's **thought life.**

The thought war is real. Listen to Paul:

 "For the weapons of our warfare are not of the flesh, but divinely powerful for the destruction of fortresses. We are destroying speculations and every lofty thing raised up against the knowledge of God, and we are taking captive EVERY THOUGHT to the obedience of Christ" (2 Cor. 10:4, 5).

"Dealing with the Devil" focuses on the believer's resistance, his SATANWARD ACTION. Since it is ACTIVE-RESISTANCE, we are most concerned with the action weapon. The only AGGRESSIVE WEAPON mentioned in Ephesians Six is . . . "the sword of the Spirit, the Word of God" (Vs. 17b).

Now a sword is designed to kill, hurt, destroy. Obviously it is not used on God. God is not the enemy of the Christian, neither are lost souls. There is only one person on whom the Word should be used as a weapon — SATAN. My concern in this book is teaching Christians **how to use** God's Word as a WEAPON. This is what is new to most. The average Christian has heard plenty of teaching on faith, truth, righteousness, etc. and if not, many noble men of the Word have exposed it beautifully already. This book is addressed to one thing . . . anti-Satan action . . . and for that, the SWORD requires our attention. It is the ONLY aggressive weapon of the Christian.

5 **"Does a ritualistic use of Jesus' name have any kind of a magical effect upon Satan . . . or his demons?"**

ANSWER: Some believe that reciting Jesus' name or other noble phrases from the Bible conjures a mystical power which drives Satan away. But this is pure superstition. Some would even rebuke the devil all the while uttering Jesus' name as a formula and reciting the words . . . "the blood of Christ," as if those very words had a magic of their own. But they do not. The use of FORMULAS for dispatching the devil or his demons is a modern form of superstition. If formulas could put Satan to flight or discharge demons, we'd have the hospitals of our land emptied in a day. And Christians would be living unhindered lives. But alas, neither is happening.

In Acts 19:13, Jewish exorcists witnessed the miraculous cures of Paul and saw that he did so in Jesus' name. They sought to do the same by employing a RITUALISTIC use of Jesus' name. They were letter-perfect in the formula, but had no power. They had absolutely no awareness of the presence of Christ in them, hence could not operate in His power. The demon, in this case, was unimpressed and prompted the victim to turn on the sons of Sceva, routing them and tearing off their clothes.

The incident shows that exorcising the demons is a matter of faith in Jesus and ACTING in that faith. It is purely a matter of faith and obedience, not ritual or recitation. It is as one has NO POWER IN HIMSELF, but behaves as a servant of Jesus, that spiritual power is manifest. Consequently it is not JESUS' NAME we use, but the power of His indwelling PRESENCE. There is a big difference.

When Christ invites us to do mighty things in His name, He is not giving us a FORMULA, but **AUTHORITY**. We are **authorized** to do things OURSELVES in the power of the Holy Spirit. It is a matter of moving in power, not reciting magical words. For example, we are authorized to go directly to God with prayer requests. The point: WE GO, WE ASK, because we have the **authority** to do so. Prayer in Jesus' name is not a formula with His title tacked on the end, but a **privilege to be exercised.**

So with resisting Satan. WE DO IT. The name of Jesus is our AUTHORITY for doing so. The Holy Spirit is our STRENGTH. The Word of God our WEAPON. The shed blood of Christ is our GUARANTEE of victory. Satan is ALREADY a defeated enemy on the basis of that blood. So we don't plead it, we don't recite it, we don't even use it . . . **we** are victorious BECAUSE OF IT! To resist Satan on the BASIS of JESUS' BLOOD is to understand that one is certain to triumph over him even as he USES THE SWORD!

When I use "in Jesus' name" in my own resisting dialogue, it is not as a weapon or formula, neither is it an incantation to scare off evil spirits. It is merely a reminder that Satan has no fear of me personally. It speaks of my helplessness apart from Jesus. It cautions against foolish pride. It declares that ONLY IN JESUS is there any victory or deliverance.

I suggest that we all use the phrase "in Jesus' name" when first starting out with the anti-Satan skill, for those first skirmishes. It not only reminds us of our dependence on Jesus, but it makes for confidence. It feels good to have His name on our lips as we face the adversary. There is an assurance that comes with it. But in time, say 3 to 6 months, it would be well to drop the phrase . . . at least make a point of NOT using it every time. That will keep you from letting it degenerate into an incantation or supposedly magical formula.

6 **"I find it hard to accept the fact that Satan can read my mind, that he is actually present to my thoughts."**

ANSWER: Then of course, you won't bother to resist him. You will find yourself resisting temptation rather than the tempter. And that is awesome, if not futile for most of us. The Word makes it clear that Satan is the "god of this world" with the power to BLIND minds. A mind-blinder has to be able to READ minds, else how can he obstruct thinking (2 Cor. 4:4)?

Jesus commented on this with perfect clarity . . . **"When anyone heareth the Word and understandeth it not, then cometh the wicked one and taketh away that which was sown in his heart"** (Matt. 13:19).

How is this possible? Where does one have to BE and what must he SEE in order to know what you DON'T UNDERSTAND? What is your understanding, if not your thought life? Satan must be able to ANALYZE your thinking to know WHEN and WHAT you do not understand. Beyond that, says Jesus, he can even take away the Word of God. One has to see what is going on to do such things. And to do that, he must be right there — PRESENT.

Ananias and Sapphira were Christians. But Satan knew their weakness. They bought his suggestion to keep back part of the money. He said no one would know. And no one would, had not the Spirit revealed the truth. Where did Satan have to be to know what was in their minds? How familiar was he with their natures, their greed? How was he able to get them to think this way? He had to be in on it, able to put the suggestion in their minds. Peter explains how it came about, **"Why hath Satan FILLED THINE HEART?"** But who got blamed? **"Why hast thou conceived** this thing . . . ?"** See? It is acknowledged as something they conceived, yet we know Satan engineered it (Acts 5:1-4).

Satan can do this. As the unholy spirit he employs the same processes as the Holy Spirit. He can lead, guide, and move us as surely as the Spirit of God. He not only beholds everything in our thoughts and imaginations, but he can add his own ideas, take away truth and blind. Fortunately nothing can be done against our wills. Everything he does must be approved by us. This is what makes us responsible in the end.

> **CAUTION:** Don't let theology weaken your respect for our enemy. If you feel I award too much power to Satan, don't go to the other extreme considering yourself immune to his influences. Theological ideas can make one an easy victim if they cause one to regard him improperly. I consider it risky to assume his powers any less than indicated by the verses we've cited. If we are going to err, let it be on the **SAFE SIDE** in over-estimation of the enemy. To underestimate the power of Satan could be disastrous. It is that way in any battle. So don't let theology cause you to discount the devil's ability to reach us with his suggestions.

7 "Can Satan see our defense plans and set about to thwart them?"

ANSWER: Yes. With the mental arena open to him he can behold all of our preparations and set into motion his own plans for countering them. But remember, his attacks are by way of **suggestion only.** Consequently some will read this book and the thought will strike . . . "I don't need that. I'm safe in Christ! Satan can't touch

191

me." Or again he plants the idea . . . "Why should Satan pay any attention to little old me?" You can see what would happen once a Christian accepted such notions. He wouldn't prepare. So indeed, Satan can plant counter-suggestions that will keep Christians from preparing themselves or bothering with the anti-Satan skill.

It might be asked, "Does it weaken our resistance to have him see our defense plans, knowing we are going to use the Word as a weapon?" NO. Because Satan sees our plans does not make God's Word any less effective, anymore than the sight of the frontiersman's six-gun on his hip made it useless. It is more likely that Satan will leave the prepared Christians alone. No one really wants to tangle with a "fast gun," not even Satan. Communist insight to our defense plans, does not make our missiles any less dreadful.

Our danger lies not in Satan's ability to view our preparations, but our **relaxed vigilance.** It is in unguarded moments, when we're occupying with some wordly item or reacting to some unpleasantness, that we are vulnerable. All of our preparation means little when our guard is down. That is Satan's advantage. He's watching for those **unguarded moments.**

Keep in mind that Satan is limited to suggestion. Seeing our plans gives him no real advantage, for it does not affect the power of God's Word. But he does see our vulnerability and knows when to strike. That's his advantage. Even so, every suggestion he deposits must still be approved by our wills. We are never the unwilling victim of the devil.

8 **"Can a study like this lead to pre-occupation with the devil?"**

ANSWER: Yes, and it should, for a time. Every time we learn anything new, there is a span of pre-occupation while we learn. Soul-winning is like that. Prophecy students have to fight to keep from going off the deep end and becoming date setters. Language students go around memorizing vocabulary in deepest concentration. You don't dare learn to fly a plane without total occupation with what you're doing. Well, a car is the same way. But the pre-occupation diminishes with driving experience.

The same applies to acquiring the anti-Satan skill. There is a pre-occupation interval while we are getting acquainted with our victory in Christ. It's exciting, refreshing and certainly consuming. There is almost a transforming effect in the life as the power of God's Word takes on this new dimension.

But it doesn't last long. Once you have the skill, Satanology drops to its rightful place in your life. It is much like the brakes on your car. Once you know how to use them, you forget them until you need them. When suddenly they are needed, you apply them IN-STINCTIVELY . . . and fast. You concentrate on driving the car, but use your brakes by instinct. And so with the anti-Satan skill. We occupy with Jesus. He is our life. Serving Him our business. But we do have an enemy and when he strikes, we react . . . INSTINCT-IVELY.

This is why we install the detection idea. It works like a burglar alarm. A jewelry store is interested in its customers and selling its jewels. That's its business. But let that alarm go off and a possible burglary becomes the new interest center. Now we're not Satan-conscious people. We are Christ-conscious. But we must post a guard. We're in a war. Our enemy lives. When the alarm rings we act. But for the most part our hands are full doing our Master's work. You will find that once you become comfortable in your resistance of the devil, his prominence subsides and you can occupy with Jesus as never before.

9 "Should young people be taught to resist the the devil?"

ANSWER. Absolutely and let's have no argument about it. When? About the time they learn to do something WITH Jesus, they should learn to do something ABOUT the devil. It is dangerous to allow youngsters to grow up thinking the Christian life is devotional only. They have a vicious enemy who lives to destroy them. They should learn of him as soon as possible.

We are admonished to be "good soldiers of Jesus Christ" (2 Tim. 2:3, 4), which confirms this life is indeed a war. Such a notion as "Come to Christ and everything will be fine," is deadly. Usually the opposite is true. The Christian life is tough. It is not for cowards or weaklings. It is for soldiers. "Watch," and "resist," and "stand fast," and "fight," are strategic words of Christianity. There is a military side. The call to Christ is also a call to active duty. If we don't teach our children how to FIGHT, they'll fall before this monster without mercy.

To let them feel immune to satanic attack because they have received the Lord, is to grant them false security. To withhold from them the instruction and equipment for Christian warfare is to make them helpless victims. They are sure to be putty in Satan's hand. Love for Jesus is not anti-satan protection. There is no such thing as AUTOMATIC victory over the devil. It is clearly a fight.

Satan has an easy time when those fiery drives awaken in young bodies. His suggestions appeal to those newly awakened feelings. He knows exactly how to harness that spirit of independence the moment it rises. Witness the wholesale exodus from church as young people enter their teens. See how he uses those appetites to lure them from spiritual things. Your family altar and preaching are powerless in the face of it. If they haven't learned how to recognize Satan's suggestions by the time they are 12 or 13 . . . and deal with them . . . it is unlikely they will go on to a real stand in Christ. I can't believe any Christian parent would willingly permit satanic disaster to strike his child when it was within his power to prevent it.

10 "Can a person read this book, start resisting Satan and expect immediate results?"

ANSWER: Yes. And the more childlike his faith, the more certain the results will be dramatic and startling. But not everyone comes to a new phase in his life in such a fashion. For some it will be a matter of cautious experimentation. Others may have doubts about the whole thing. And some, of course, will read the book to approve it theologically, and do nothing about it.

How secure one is in the Word and the measure of his faith, both in the power of the Holy Spirit and the reality of Satan, determine the kind of success he will have with this plan. It is much like one's first experiences in prayer. Often it is a new life, strange, leaving you wondering if God really hears. Yet it becomes unquestioned in time. However, should God's answer to your very first prayer request be speedy and dramatic, you are off to a great start in the prayer life. It is not always that way. For many it is the slower process of developing confidence in Him and His invitation to come with requests.

So with the anti-Satan skill. If your first attempt results in a spectacular victory and Satan's flight is so moving it leaves you almost breathless, you're off to a new life of victory in Christ. But if your first attempts are puzzling, you're filled with doubt and not sure of any release, your assurance will have to come more slowly. It is important that you give yourself time to develop the necessary confidence in God's Word and the Spirit's willingness to empower you against Satan. It will come. In time you will be dealing as certainly with the devil, to dispatch him, as you do with God to worship Him!

Don't sell yourself or this plan short by too quick a judgment. Don't be too fast to say, "I tried that and it didn't work." Give yourself a bit of time. Refuse to give up because of a few defeats and you won't be sorry. Before long you'll have as much confidence in resisting Satan as you do in serving Jesus.

11 "Do Christians tend to be superstitious about Satan?"

ANSWER: Yes. Some even feel chills when his name is mentioned in a discussion. Others won't talk about him. They fear retaliation, much as the heathen fear snakes and lightning and worship them. Why such superstition in those who are born-again? Ignorance does to Christians what it does to anyone else. It breeds superstition. Some preachers won't preach on him for fear trouble will follow. They laugh at voodoo and witchcraft, yet behave in similar fashion about the devil. Satan has exploited this ignorance and uses superstitious fear to keep Christians from learning of the authority they have over him in Christ.

Should you announce a class on Satanology, don't be shocked if a group should come to you and say, "Let us know when it is over and we'll be back."

12 "You hear about the world, the flesh and the devil. Does this mean we have three enemies, instead of one?"

ANSWER: Satan is the god of this world and he is thoroughly familiar with the weakness of our flesh. It is popular to say we have three enemies, but this just is not so. We have only ONE enemy, but he USES the world and our flesh as the weapons of his warfare against us. The world offers men THINGS. Man's flesh RESPONDS to the things of this world. Without these Satan would have nothing to use against us.

Picture the process like this: Satan knows our flesh loves the things of the world. He deposits ideas in our minds which cause us to lust after the things of the world, long for them as we think how nice it would be to have them, scheme to get them, occupy with them once we have them and finally take pride in them. Satan is our enemy, but he uses the WORLD and our FLESH as weapons. See it like this:

> The WORLD is bait
> It appeals to our FLESH
> The DEVIL lures us to take the bait.

If we can successfully resist his suggestions, the world and the flesh cannot compete with the attractiveness of Christ. It is only as Satan uses the world and our flesh that they have any force. It is merely because he can deceive us with his enticing suggestions that they have any appeal to a born-again Christian.

13 "When we entertain EVIL in our minds, to what degree do those thoughts originate with us, or is Satan always the author?"

Answer: Satan always has a part in our evil. There is never a time when we're not subject to his influence. He's at home in our old nature. His eyes are never off our thought-stream. He bombards our thinking with a steady stream. Listen to what God says about our old natures:

'And God saw that the wickedness of man was great

197

in the earth and that EVERY IMAGINATION of the thoughts of his heart was only evil continually" (Gen 6:5).

Nothing has changed since that was written.

"The heart is deceitful ABOVE ALL THINGS and desperately wicked, who can know it?" (Jer. 17:9).

When you have a nature like that, and we all do, evil is being pressed on us continually. No one has to dream up evil. When we come to Christ and receive the NEW NATURE, an opposite situation is created. The Holy Spirit is continually prompting us to do what pleases God (righteousness). With our FREE WILLS, we can choose which of these opposing forces we will surrender to. **But that's as far as our freedom goes.** The truth is, WE'RE SLAVES, either of righteousness or sin (Rom. 6:16). Therefore all the EVIL we tolerate in our minds, has its source in Satan. And all the righteousness we entertain, has its source in God's Spirit. The question asks: to what "degree" do those thoughts originate with us? The specific answer: to the degree to which we yield to the old nature. Since we are free to choose which nature will dominate our lives, we're responsible for what occurs in our minds. But as for our generating evil ourselves, that's not necessary. It's already done for us.

NOTE: The above question deals with EVIL ONLY and should not be understood to mean we never have ANY THOUGHTS OF OUR OWN. Of course we do. We are made in the image of a THINKER AND CREATOR and as such, we're capable of independent thinking and creating. For example, it is independent thinking that visualized a bridge across San Francisco Bay and planned a space flight to the moon. But when it comes to the areas of EVIL and RIGHTEOUSNESS . . . and those two areas alone . . . we are NOT ABLE to think independently. In those two arenas, God and Satan run the show. Those two majesties are continually offering temptation on the one hand, and inspiration on the other.

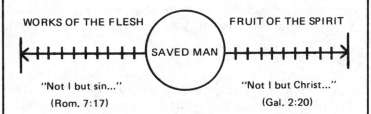

THE CHRISTIAN'S SURRENDER TO BOTH NATURES

WORKS OF THE FLESH   FRUIT OF THE SPIRIT

SAVED MAN

"Not I but sin..."   "Not I but Christ..."
(Rom. 7:17)   (Gal. 2:20)

Whereas the unsaved man was able, in degree, to surrender to the old nature only, the believer is capable of surrender in two directions. He can do God-pleasing works (righteousness) through the "Spirit of Christ." He can also do evil works of the flesh through the "spirit of disobedience." The degree to which he surrenders to either spirit, is the degree he will manifest either of his two natures.

14 "I find I'm not getting anywhere with my continual resistance of Satan, and I'm afraid I'm going to give in before he does. Is there anything else I can do besides ordering him away every time?

Answer: Good question. Christians are not used to fighting. Oh, they'll keep it up for a time, but the devil knows from experience they'll cave in if he comes back often enough. Not all Christians are willing to "tough it out," and the devil knows it. But there is another technique for dealing with him which is very powerful. If you find yourself on the verge of giving up, here's another way to win.

The technique I'm about to describe exploits the devil's BIG EGO. He has a HUGE EGO and it's his weak spot. We can use it against him. Here's how it works:

We'll assume you have a health problem. Some tumors

199

the size of ping-pong balls have been found on your thyroid gland. The very thought of CANCER sends chills down your spine, much to Satan's glee. With the doctors not too encouraging, Satan easily attacks you with fear and worry. You hate that, because you know it hurts the Lord when you don't really trust Him.

Here comes Satan.

You're doing a routine job around the house. Day-dreaming perhaps. A hospital scene pops into your mind. You see yourself in bed with doctors all around and terrible fears surge through your spirit. You shake off the dream. "Ah ha! Satan's back!" You now have him in your trap. But instead of ordering him away, as you usually do, you say to him...

"Thank you Satan for attacking me. Your attack reminds me to praise the Lord. In fact, every time you attack me about this cancer business, I'm going to accept it as a SIGNAL to praise the Lord. From now on, I'm going to use every one of your attacks to remind me of the Lord's kindness and minister to Him."

You use the next few moments to go into the "secret place" and share yourself with Jesus, lavishing your love and praise on Him — **with Satan watching.** You're now worshipping the Lord SOLELY because the devil attacked you. *

What will Satan do then?

---

*If you do not know how to go into the "secret place" and hold Jesus in your arms, a super thrill awaits you when you read my book, **LONGING TO BE LOVED.** It gives step-by-step instructions for entering the secret place and feeling at home with Jesus. It will fill you with great joy and reinforce your determination to put Satan to flight.

FUME! He'll turn red . . . then white . . then blue with rage. He'll bang his fists against the wall, steam gushing from his ears! Grinding his teeth, he'll go stomping from the scene. It drives him crazy to have you turn his attacks against him like this. It tears him apart to have his work bring glory to Jesus, but that's what's just happened. This is a PAINFUL THRUST, the worst kind for the devil. Big egoes, you see, can't take this kind of pain. It's the worst possible put-down.

Let the devil receive this kind of treatment from you a few times, and he'll back off to lick his wounds. It'll be some time before he attacks you with CANCER WORRY again. You've now stood up to him — WON! And if you lavish yourself on the Lord . . . right before Satan's eyes . . . because he attacked you, you can't imagine what the devil suffers. Total devastation. Don't think it isn't fun to turn the tables on him like this, especially after the abuse you've been receiving at his hands.

NOTE. In this illustration I used WORRY over health as Satan's weapon. But it could just as easily been LUST or a NASTY HABIT of some kind. Maybe RESENTMENT, JEALOUSY or a BROKEN HEART . . . even FINANCIAL DISTRESS. It doesn't matter what kind of a problem Satan uses to torment you, you can TORMENT HIM with this technique. When he sees his attacks sending you into the Lord's presence, and Jesus lapping up all that praise and affection—it kills him to think he's responsible. Hating Jesus as he does, it makes him sick to see it. Without argument, this kind of KNOWLEDGE IS POWER.

LIKE TO GET INVOLVED WITH THE AUTHOR?

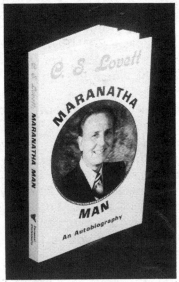

No. 548

Now that you have read **Dealing With The Devil**, used the plan and find that it works, you may wish to know more about the author and become personally involved in the vision of preparing Christians for our Lord's appearing. To become involved, read Dr. Lovett's exciting autobiography telling how the Lord inspired him to be his **maranatha man,** and God's plan for your helping to fulfill the vision.

(To order **Maranatha Man**, see next page. Write for catalog.)

FOR THE TEACHER

An exciting manual for action packed classes. Photos show simulated actions and how to use props. Every detail for a class on resisting the devil, showing precisely how to transfer the skill. Ideal for groups. Recommended for ages 12 years and up.

No. 532 ▪ TEACH THEM ABOUT SATAN (Teacher's Guide for Dealing With The Devil)—By C. S. Lovett

---

ABOUT THE AUTHOR. . .DR. C. S. LOVETT

Dr. Lovett is the president of **Personal Christianity,** a fundamental, evangelical interdenominational ministry. For the past 33 years he has had but one objective—**preparing Christians for the second coming of Christ!** This book is one of over 40 of his works designed to help believers **prepare for His appearing.**

Dr. Lovett's decision to serve the Lord resulted in the loss of a sizable personal fortune. He is well equipped for the job the Lord has given him. A graduate of American Baptist Seminary of the West, He holds the M.A. and M. Div. degrees conferred *Magna Cum Laude.* He has also completed graduate work in psychology at Los Angeles State College and holds an honorary doctorate from the Protestant Episcopal University in London.

A retired Air Force Chaplain (Lt. Colonel), he has been married to Marjorie for over 42 years and has two grown daughters dedicated to the Lord.